Advance Praise

"First of all, [I like *American Sentences*] because they're extremely vivid & detail-oriented, a la the haiku. Emphasis is on the image, rather than rhetoric, or lyricism. Unlike the haiku, however, which is a highly bastardized form in English, they're more suited to the American idiom & so allow a greater range of natural expression. They don't have the aesthetic stiffness of the haiku as they are practiced in English.

I also really like your sense of wit & humor ("the Australian kiss, kissing down under"), or the occasional non-sequitur, a giant ear popping out of nowhere."

—John Olson, author of numerous books of poetry, including *Larynx Galaxy* and *Backscatter: New and Selected Poems* and three novels, including *The Seeing Machine, The Nothing That Is*, and *Souls of Wind*, the latter of which was shortlisted for a Believer book of the year award in 2008.

Dedicated to my love, Bhakti Watts

American Sentences Introduction to Second Edition

Another day comes and goes and with it all the daily rituals. On a good day there is journaling, yoga, prayers and divination before breakfast. Hopefully there is some dream recall and some clues as to the aspects of shadow that block the path to individuation. And for over twenty years there has been a daily 17 syllable poem. An American Sentence.

I became familiar with the form when I read *Cosmopolitan Greetings* by Allen Ginsberg while preparing to interview him June 12, 1994. In that book are the poems that his colleagues at Naropa University (then the Naropa Institute) talked about when I interviewed them in 2001. About the form, Anne Waldman and Andrew Schelling told me:

> Andrew Schelling: Well, based on haiku, which Allen loved the idea that it was 17 syllables, but he was also very interested, of course, in Buddhism for the second half of his life. Probably the central mantra, or wisdom phrase, of Buddhism comes from the Heart Sutra. It runs, "Gate gate paragate parasamgate bodhi svaha." And Allen discovered that has 17 syllables also. And he felt that maybe 17 syllables had a more universal application.
>
> Anne Waldman: Healing properties.
>
> Andrew Schelling: It was not just located in Japan or old India, and so this was a way of him playing with that possibility.
>
> Paul E Nelson: Americanizing it.
>
> Anne Waldman: And well, also, of course, the Japanese line, as we were pointing out in the [SPLAB] workshop is, one line down, the characters running down the page. It's not broken up into these three neat lines as you see in translated haiku. So, the sense of that one, and also the running together of the thoughts that has the energy of the way the mind works, that actually you are putting these things together, even though they seem tripartite. And in the traditional view of the haiku, heaven, earth, man. *In the medicine cabinet, the winter fly has died of old age.*
>
> Paul E Nelson: Kerouac's haiku.
>
> Anne Waldman: Kerouac's.
>
> Andrew Schelling: And if you think of Allen's maximum information, minimum number of syllables, well, seventeen's a small number of

> syllables, so how to make a poem that really carries the weight of a poem? And I think that fascinated him and should become a form that's used regularly in workshops.

One other thing Andrew mentioned during that visit, at a talk given to students at West Auburn High School, was that a poet should always have a pocket journal. Here I sit on San Juan Island nearly a quarter of a century later next to 6 years of pocket journals filled with 17 syllable poems awaiting harvest. Every day a sentence for over 20 years (How can I stop now?). I am reminded of the wonderful anthology *Japanese Death Poems* and hope someday to have a poem written at that level of wisdom, but until then I hack away at the shadows of many moments in my life 17 syllables at a time. Sometimes 16. Sometimes 18. Always trying for something deeper than what Charles Olson called "the dodges of discourse" despite our 21st century world which continues to confuse rhetoric with poetry, and often settling for rhetoric.

Most sentences stay in the pocket journals. Most are written as reminders to myself, as journal entries, as notes related to my spiritual practice of Latihan Kedjiwaan, which would be misunderstood by a non-Subud audience that has not experienced that practice. I have watched one daughter grow up in sentences, with some life experiences captured in poems, and another be born while in the thick of my daily practice (They are already getting their revenge for this!). There is often a sweetness there only a parent would appreciate, so those poems remain private for the most part unless they have some sense of the universal. As Michael McClure said, "The way to the universal is by means of the most intensely personal," and sometimes I err on the side of the intensely personal in some of the poems in this second edition, but I lean towards the open to a fault. Please forgive me if you find something offensive or if the poems leave you confused. All of them have a story and I think that's what the best poetry does. The best poetry is a window into deep experience. Time compacted by the poet into (in American Sentences) about as short a form as possible while still remaining viable as a poem.

As the years have gone by, I stand more revealed as a half-Cuban, Chicago-born, working class Dad ensconced in the bioregion of Cascadia and the TUX woo' kwib Watershed (as the Duwamish people knew it), deeply in love, dedicated to the life of a poet as I have understood it. A life where good fortune has allowed me to engage with so many poets who also lived that poet's life, among them those noted above, along with Sam Hamill, Wanda Coleman, Ian Boyden, José Kozer, Joanne Kyger, Brenda Hillman, Nate Mackey, Daphne Marlatt, George Bowering, Sharon Thesen, Barry McKinnon, Judith Roche, John Olson, CA Conrad, Matt Trease, Cate Gable,

Eileen Myles, Peter Munro, Sharon Thesen, Rob Lewis, Nadine Maestas, Adelia MacWilliam, Pablo Baler, Ramón Gómez de la Serna, Jared Leising, Robin Blaser, Meredith Nelson, Chuck Pirtle, Carolyne Wright, Adelia MacWilliam, and many, many others, along with translators, journalists, musicians and philosophers like Jason Wirth, Rebecca Nelson, Jim O'Halloran, Hamilton Cheifetz, Dan Blunck, Denis Mair and Bill Porter. May some of their genius be transmitted to you.

2001

1.2.01 – Alternating oil massage, we decide against greasing up the cat.

2.1.01 – Coronas reflect off Trane's horn exposing universe's beauty.

2.3.01 – 12 vehicle crash northbound I-5 caused by slick roads & a rainbow.

2.6.01 – In right-wing Senator's office, framed picture of the Enola Gay.

2.9.01 – One small spat & you reconstruct front room into bedroom-in-exile.

3.6.01 – Former war planner Dick Cheney in hospital to clear his blocked heart.

3.15.01 – Lines out double-doors @ the post office but Carol doesn't seem to mind.

4.13.01 – Five months after election, barnyard sign says: *Slade Gorton works for me.*

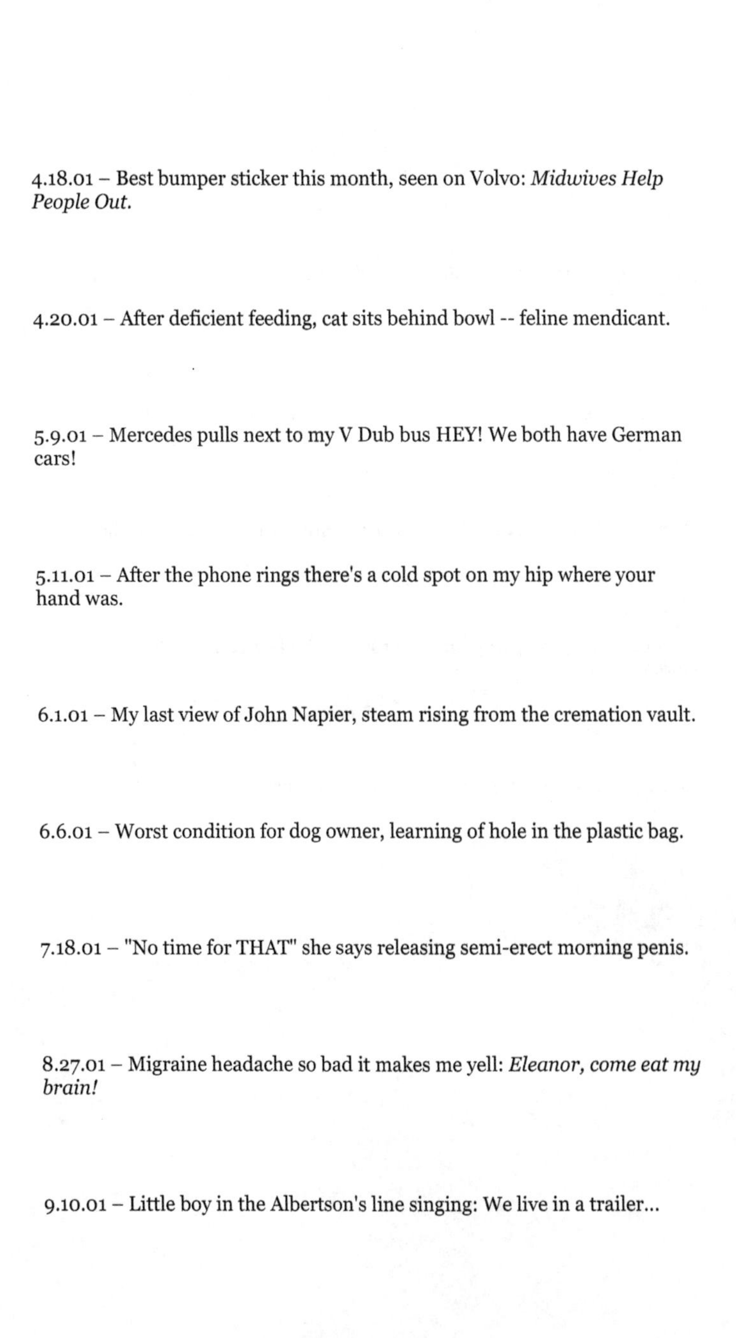

4.18.01 – Best bumper sticker this month, seen on Volvo: *Midwives Help People Out.*

4.20.01 – After deficient feeding, cat sits behind bowl -- feline mendicant.

5.9.01 – Mercedes pulls next to my V Dub bus HEY! We both have German cars!

5.11.01 – After the phone rings there's a cold spot on my hip where your hand was.

6.1.01 – My last view of John Napier, steam rising from the cremation vault.

6.6.01 – Worst condition for dog owner, learning of hole in the plastic bag.

7.18.01 – "No time for THAT" she says releasing semi-erect morning penis.

8.27.01 – Migraine headache so bad it makes me yell: *Eleanor, come eat my brain!*

9.10.01 – Little boy in the Albertson's line singing: We live in a trailer...

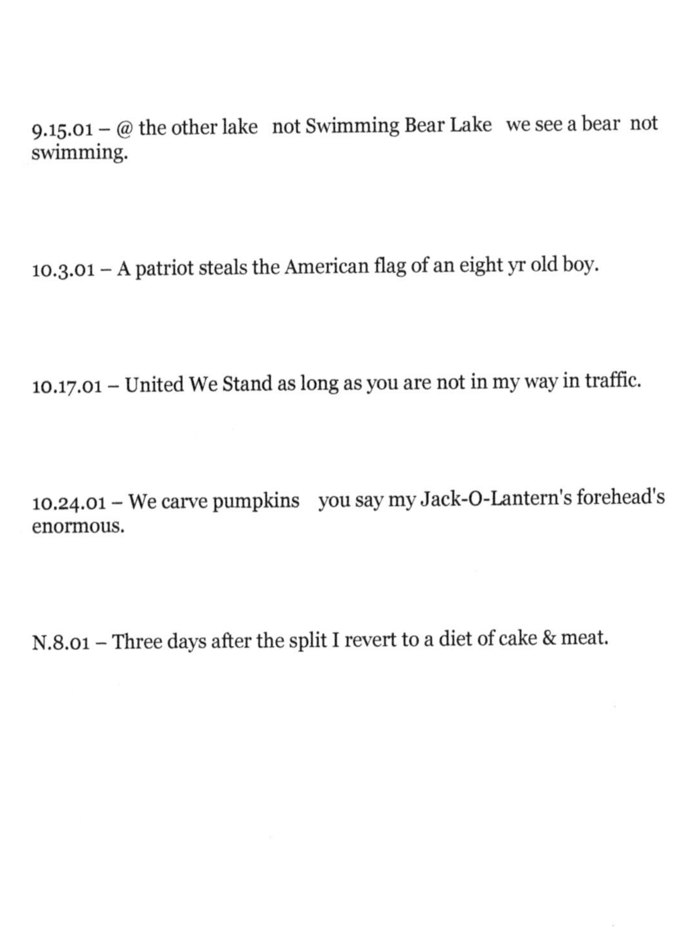

9.15.01 – @ the other lake   not Swimming Bear Lake   we see a bear not swimming.

10.3.01 – A patriot steals the American flag of an eight yr old boy.

10.17.01 – United We Stand as long as you are not in my way in traffic.

10.24.01 – We carve pumpkins   you say my Jack-O-Lantern's forehead's enormous.

N.8.01 – Three days after the split I revert to a diet of cake & meat.

2002

2.8.02 – Next to condom dispenser is written: This is the worst gum ever.

2.22.02 – Poetry reading interrupted by *Mexican Hat Dance* on a CELLPHONE!

3.10.02 – Shimmer of the hot springs pool as reflections of raindrops intersect.

4.19.02 – Canada's flag half mast past the Peace Arch from our friendly fire.

4.20.02 – Behind END ISRAEL OCCUPATION rally, kosher hot dog stand.

6.6.02 – In charred bus after suicide bomb two corpses in one last embrace.

6.12.02 – Only thing wrong w/ love poems is that the poem outlasts the love.

6.22.02 – Man who sprays Round-Up on his lawn complains when my dog pisses on it.

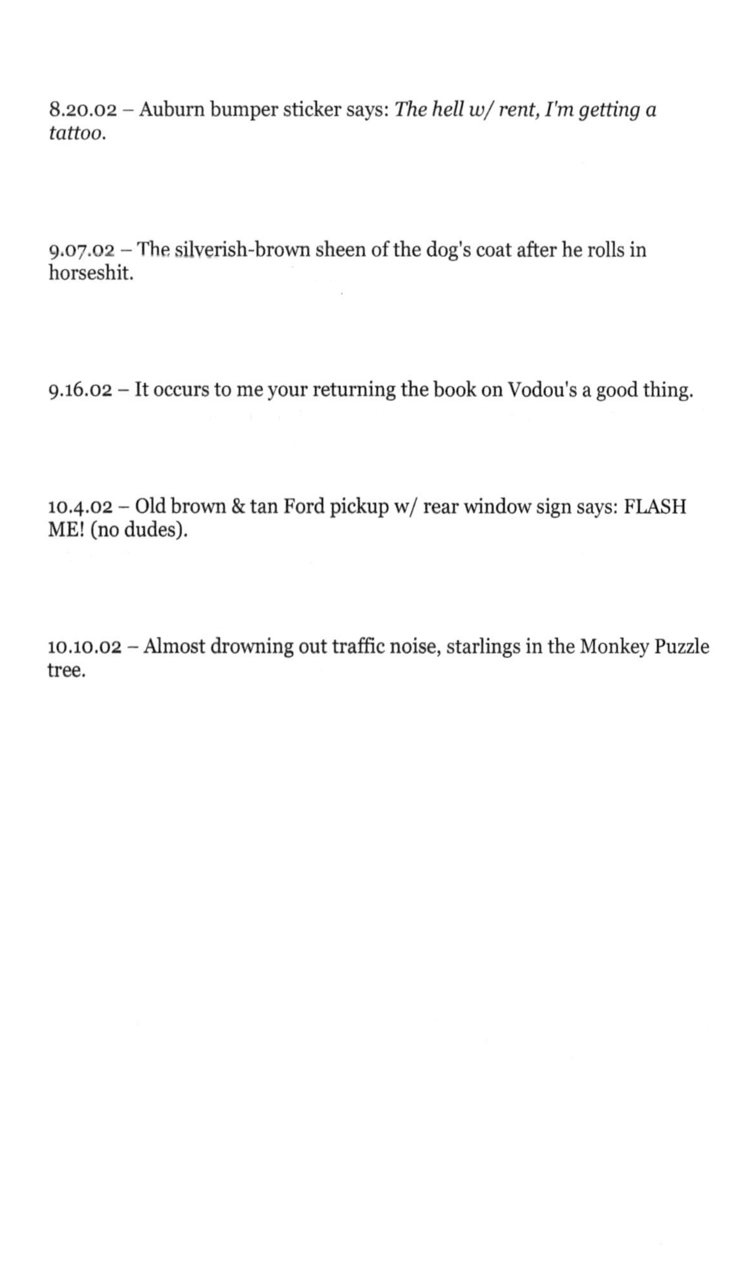

8.20.02 – Auburn bumper sticker says: *The hell w/ rent, I'm getting a tattoo.*

9.07.02 – The silverish-brown sheen of the dog's coat after he rolls in horseshit.

9.16.02 – It occurs to me your returning the book on Vodou's a good thing.

10.4.02 – Old brown & tan Ford pickup w/ rear window sign says: FLASH ME! (no dudes).

10.10.02 – Almost drowning out traffic noise, starlings in the Monkey Puzzle tree.

2003

1.23.03 – Mom's advice translated poorly: *The stars incline but they do not force.*

1.26.03 – *Aside from the potential poisoning did you enjoy dinner?*

2.1.03 – 1st Israeli astronaut immolates over Palestine, Texas.

2.20.03 – Sherry Marx reports of the peace protestor who broke a man's nose.

2.22.03 – Raphael says *why didn't they just take off the S make it Laughter?*

4.1.03 – P.O.W. freed, her home town in West Virginia Palestine.

4.7.03 – Found in Iraq: WEAPONS OF MASS DESTRUCTION or maybe pesticides.

4.9.03 – Maintenance man leaves a note says: *...can't fix your faucet its threads are striped.*

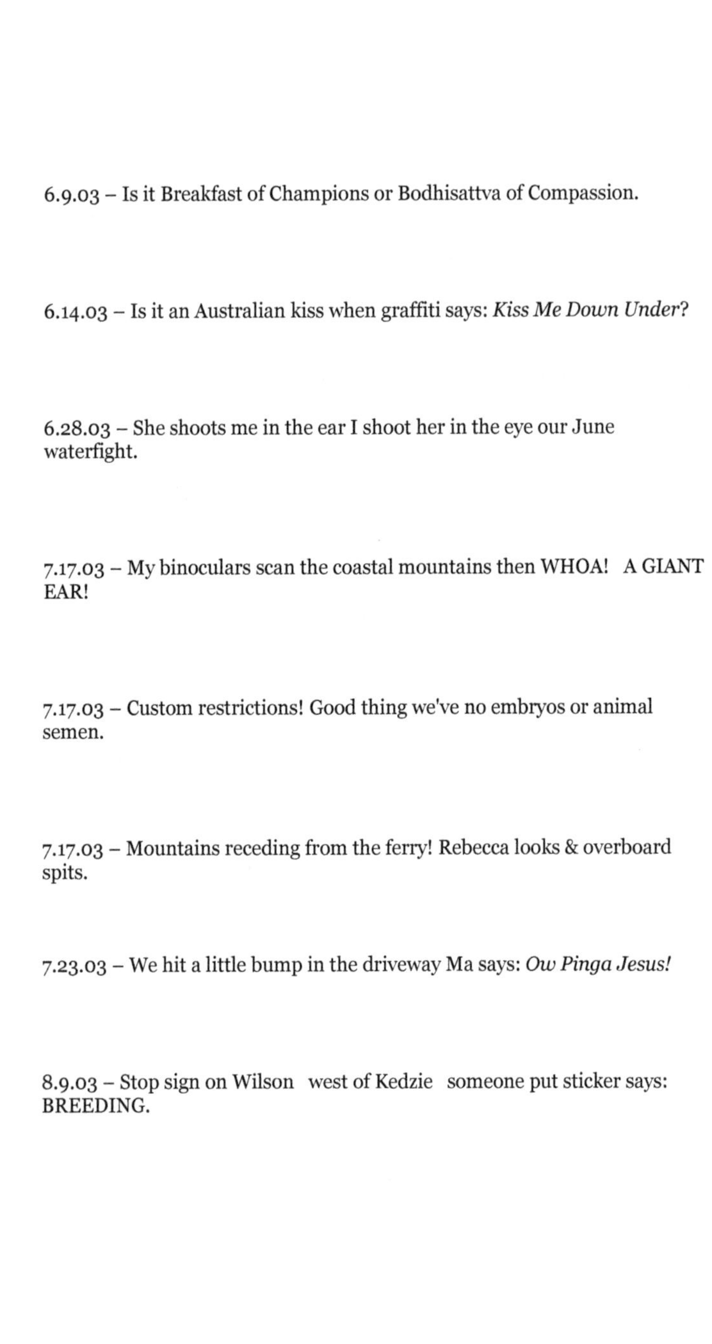

6.9.03 – Is it Breakfast of Champions or Bodhisattva of Compassion.

6.14.03 – Is it an Australian kiss when graffiti says: *Kiss Me Down Under*?

6.28.03 – She shoots me in the ear I shoot her in the eye our June waterfight.

7.17.03 – My binoculars scan the coastal mountains then WHOA!   A GIANT EAR!

7.17.03 – Custom restrictions! Good thing we've no embryos or animal semen.

7.17.03 – Mountains receding from the ferry! Rebecca looks & overboard spits.

7.23.03 – We hit a little bump in the driveway Ma says: *Ow Pinga Jesus!*

8.9.03 – Stop sign on Wilson   west of Kedzie   someone put sticker says: BREEDING.

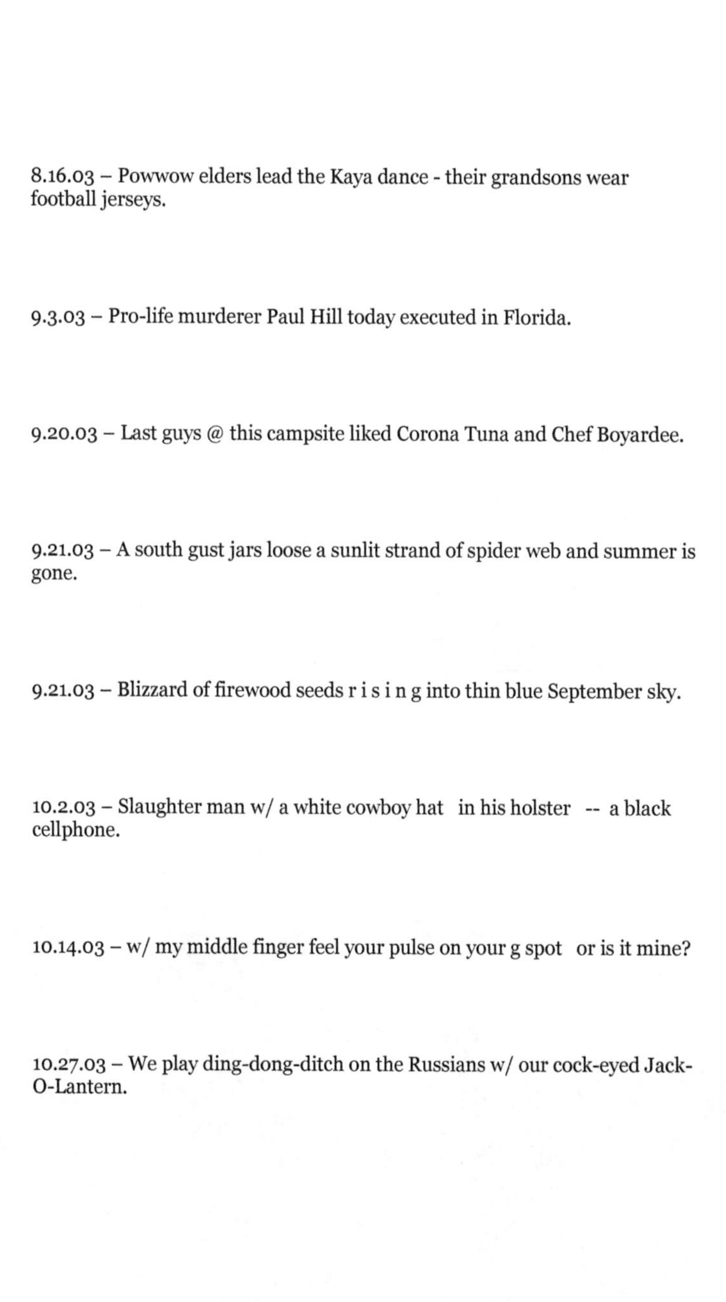

8.16.03 – Powwow elders lead the Kaya dance - their grandsons wear football jerseys.

9.3.03 – Pro-life murderer Paul Hill today executed in Florida.

9.20.03 – Last guys @ this campsite liked Corona Tuna and Chef Boyardee.

9.21.03 – A south gust jars loose a sunlit strand of spider web and summer is gone.

9.21.03 – Blizzard of firewood seeds r i s i n g into thin blue September sky.

10.2.03 – Slaughter man w/ a white cowboy hat   in his holster -- a black cellphone.

10.14.03 – w/ my middle finger feel your pulse on your g spot   or is it mine?

10.27.03 – We play ding-dong-ditch on the Russians w/ our cock-eyed Jack-O-Lantern.

N.17.03 – Our Jack-O-Lanterns were *like two old men dying in a splash of guts.*

N.22.03 – w/ serious faces they all wait outside the hospital & smoke.

N.22.03 – Almost as loud as next-door neighbor's rap – whistling of Pop's hearing aid.

2004

3.9.04 – It's a long swim to Cambodia from Hudson River Spalding Gray.

3.12.04 – After the terror bombings cellphones ring next to corpses in Madrid.

3.15.04 – They move slow around the old candy stuck to downtown sidewalk these ants.

3.17.04 – The 150 drives by on D St. & all the woodfrogs go silent.

3.21.04 – *Erections lasting 4 hours may need immediate medical help.*

4.6.04 – Cut w/ a kitchen knife Mexican self-inflicted caesarean.

4.19.04 – RR says: *I don't trust a place that does not have any refried beans.*

4.22.04 – If war happens & you don't see coffin photos is the soldier dead?

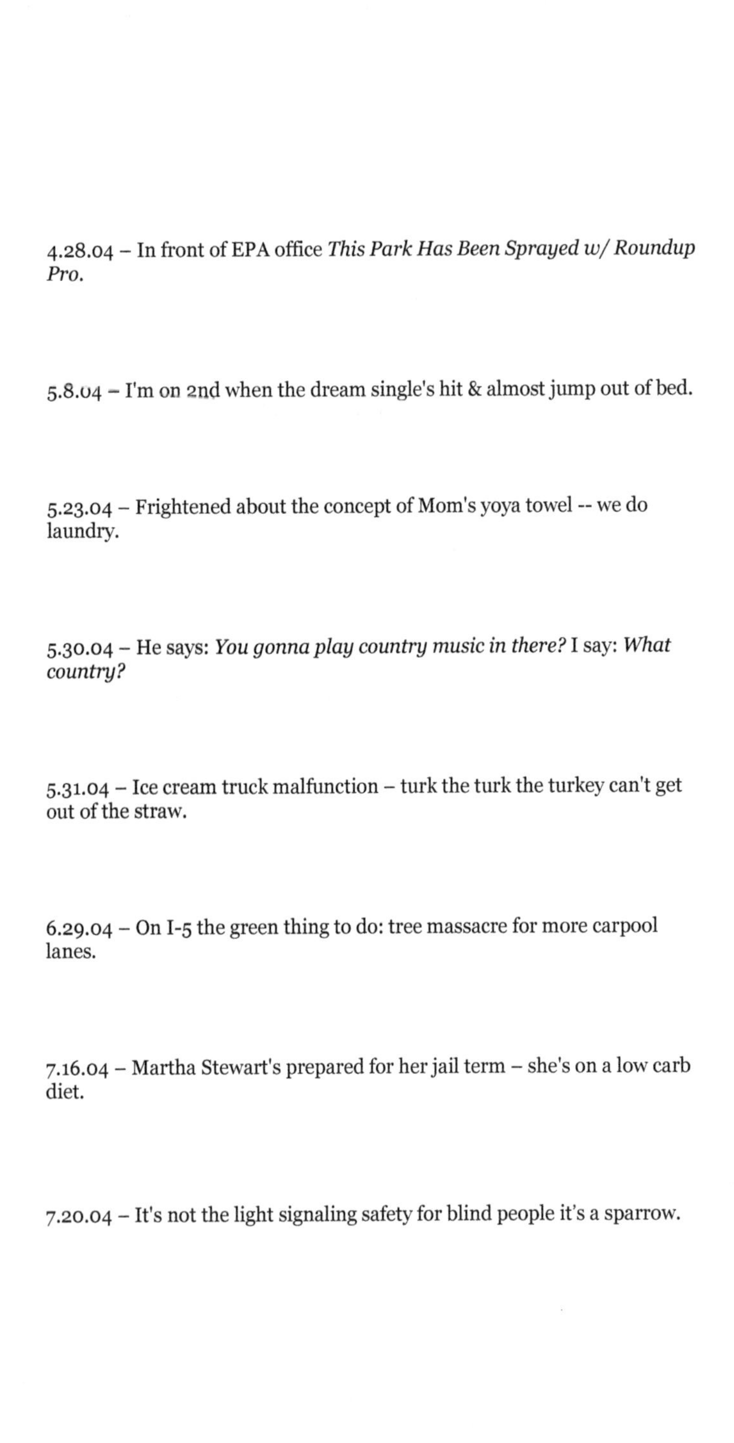

4.28.04 – In front of EPA office *This Park Has Been Sprayed w/ Roundup Pro.*

5.8.04 – I'm on 2nd when the dream single's hit & almost jump out of bed.

5.23.04 – Frightened about the concept of Mom's yoya towel -- we do laundry.

5.30.04 – He says: *You gonna play country music in there?* I say: *What country?*

5.31.04 – Ice cream truck malfunction – turk the turk the turkey can't get out of the straw.

6.29.04 – On I-5 the green thing to do: tree massacre for more carpool lanes.

7.16.04 – Martha Stewart's prepared for her jail term – she's on a low carb diet.

7.20.04 – It's not the light signaling safety for blind people it's a sparrow.

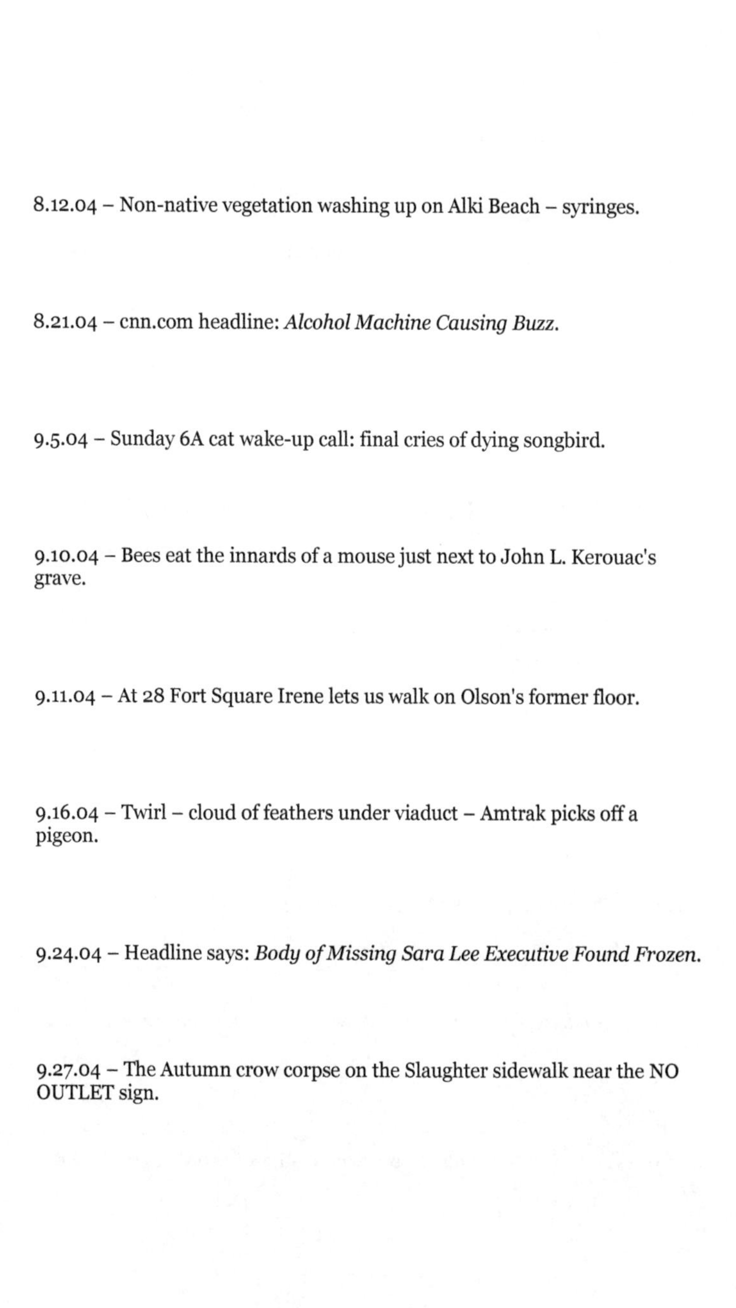

8.12.04 – Non-native vegetation washing up on Alki Beach – syringes.

8.21.04 – cnn.com headline: *Alcohol Machine Causing Buzz.*

9.5.04 – Sunday 6A cat wake-up call: final cries of dying songbird.

9.10.04 – Bees eat the innards of a mouse just next to John L. Kerouac's grave.

9.11.04 – At 28 Fort Square Irene lets us walk on Olson's former floor.

9.16.04 – Twirl – cloud of feathers under viaduct – Amtrak picks off a pigeon.

9.24.04 – Headline says: *Body of Missing Sara Lee Executive Found Frozen.*

9.27.04 – The Autumn crow corpse on the Slaughter sidewalk near the NO OUTLET sign.

2005

3.14.05 – Wanda Coleman told me she is praying Bush gets a bad pretzel.

3.17.05 – *Mind if we use your fairway?* they ask – *go ahead, we're not using it.*

3.29.05 – Charlie told us: *If you hear gurgling noises it's my leg falling off.*

3.30.05 – Blue sound-proofing foam scattered in the rubble pile – all that's left of SPLAB!

4.6.05 – Sylvester @ Kiwanis talks about Skip-a-Meal fund – mouth full of eggs.

4.12.05 – She woke him up w/ her Ramones ringtone: *I Want to be Sedated.*

4.18.05 – *Children remain the best witnesses unless someone else steps forward.*

4.21.05 – Walt Whitman – one w/ everything – I use his book to swat dead a fly.

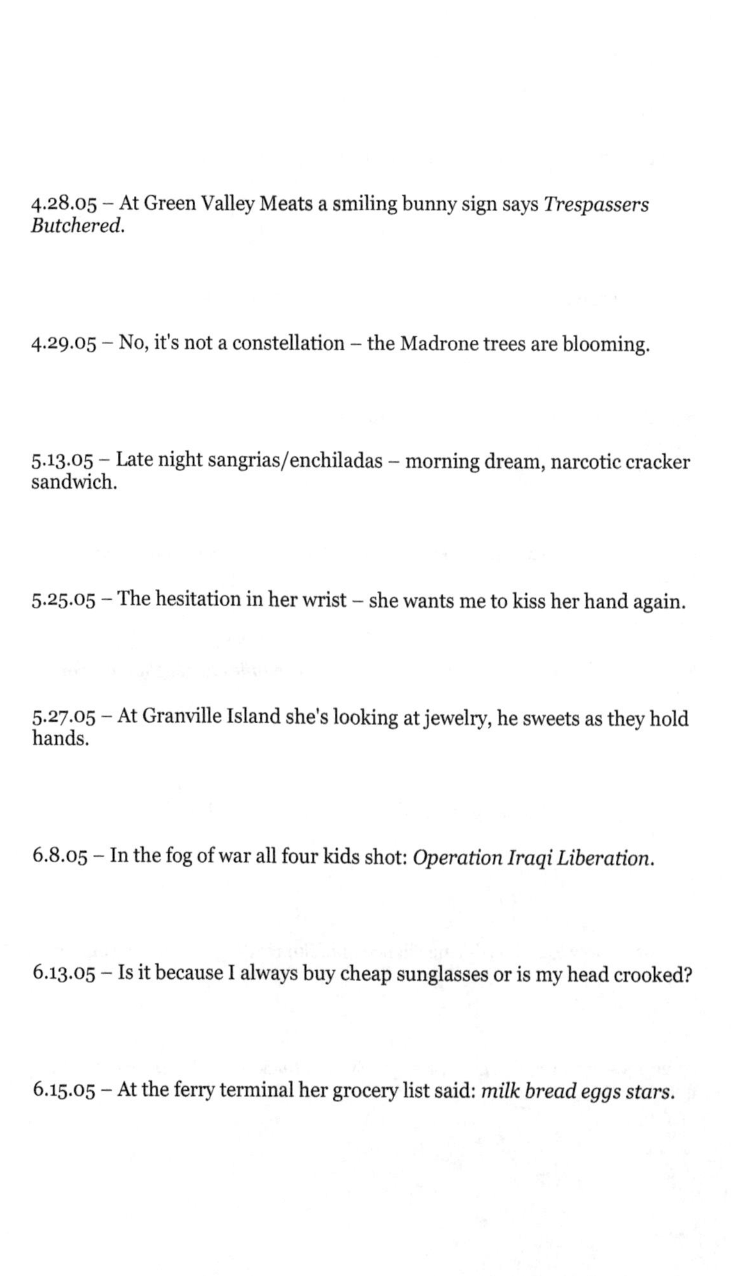

4.28.05 – At Green Valley Meats a smiling bunny sign says *Trespassers Butchered.*

4.29.05 – No, it's not a constellation – the Madrone trees are blooming.

5.13.05 – Late night sangrias/enchiladas – morning dream, narcotic cracker sandwich.

5.25.05 – The hesitation in her wrist – she wants me to kiss her hand again.

5.27.05 – At Granville Island she's looking at jewelry, he sweets as they hold hands.

6.8.05 – In the fog of war all four kids shot: *Operation Iraqi Liberation.*

6.13.05 – Is it because I always buy cheap sunglasses or is my head crooked?

6.15.05 – At the ferry terminal her grocery list said: *milk bread eggs stars.*

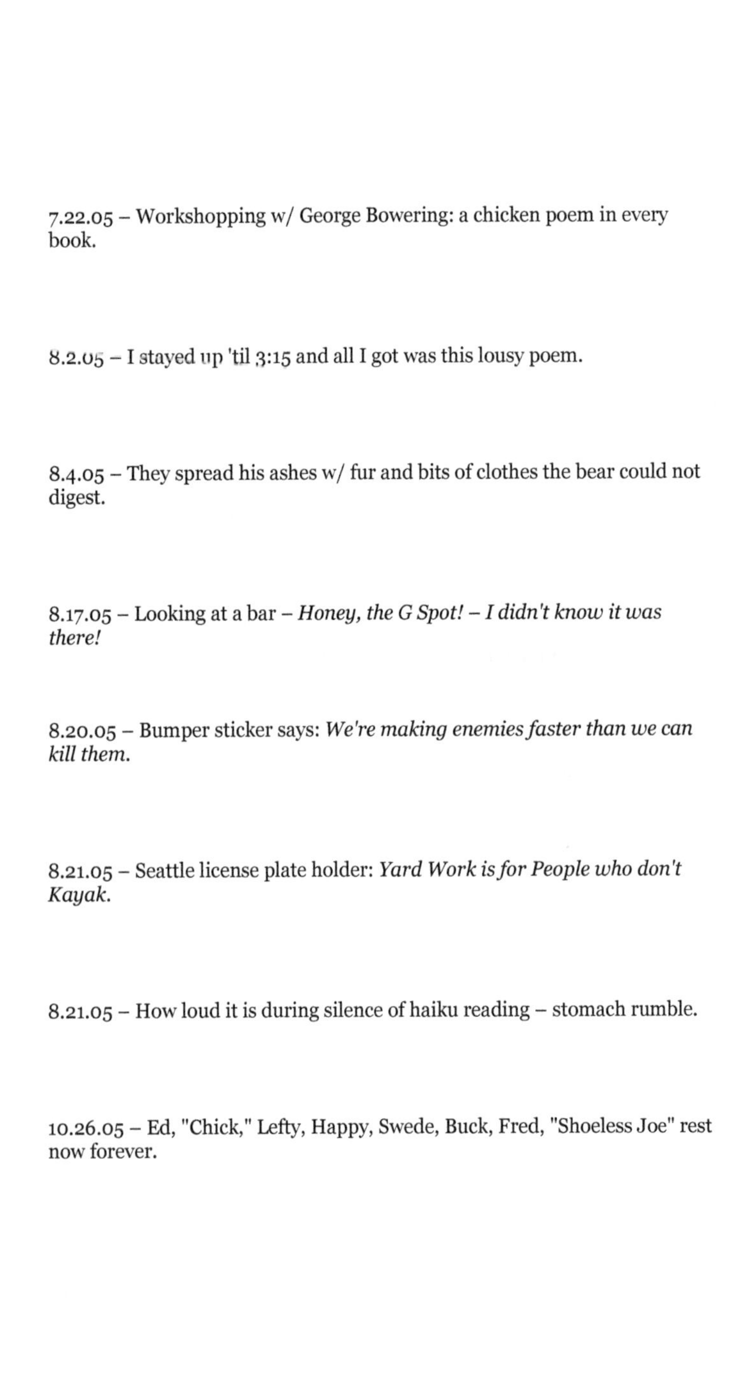

7.22.05 – Workshopping w/ George Bowering: a chicken poem in every book.

8.2.05 – I stayed up 'til 3:15 and all I got was this lousy poem.

8.4.05 – They spread his ashes w/ fur and bits of clothes the bear could not digest.

8.17.05 – Looking at a bar – *Honey, the G Spot! – I didn't know it was there!*

8.20.05 – Bumper sticker says: *We're making enemies faster than we can kill them.*

8.21.05 – Seattle license plate holder: *Yard Work is for People who don't Kayak.*

8.21.05 – How loud it is during silence of haiku reading – stomach rumble.

10.26.05 – Ed, "Chick," Lefty, Happy, Swede, Buck, Fred, "Shoeless Joe" rest now forever.

2006

1.18.06 – At the Otter Café Sam says: *Don't try the sausage, it's a little furry.*

1.26.06 – Black jetta east on 16 license plate holder says: *Can't sleep, clowns will eat me.*

2.2.06 – Northwest Groundhog pops out of his hole & sees forty more days of rain.

2.4.06 – Pop comes to town says: *Your Mother keeps that place so cold you can hang meat.*

2.15.06 – Do you remember the time when shoes lasted longer than shoelaces?

4.7.06 – Dead get stuck in yr throat in the fetal position causing you to write.

4.27.06 – Rule #6 – Never wake a sleeping man unless the room is on fire.

5.3.06 – She outgrows bedtime stories w/ assistance of her trusty I-Pod.

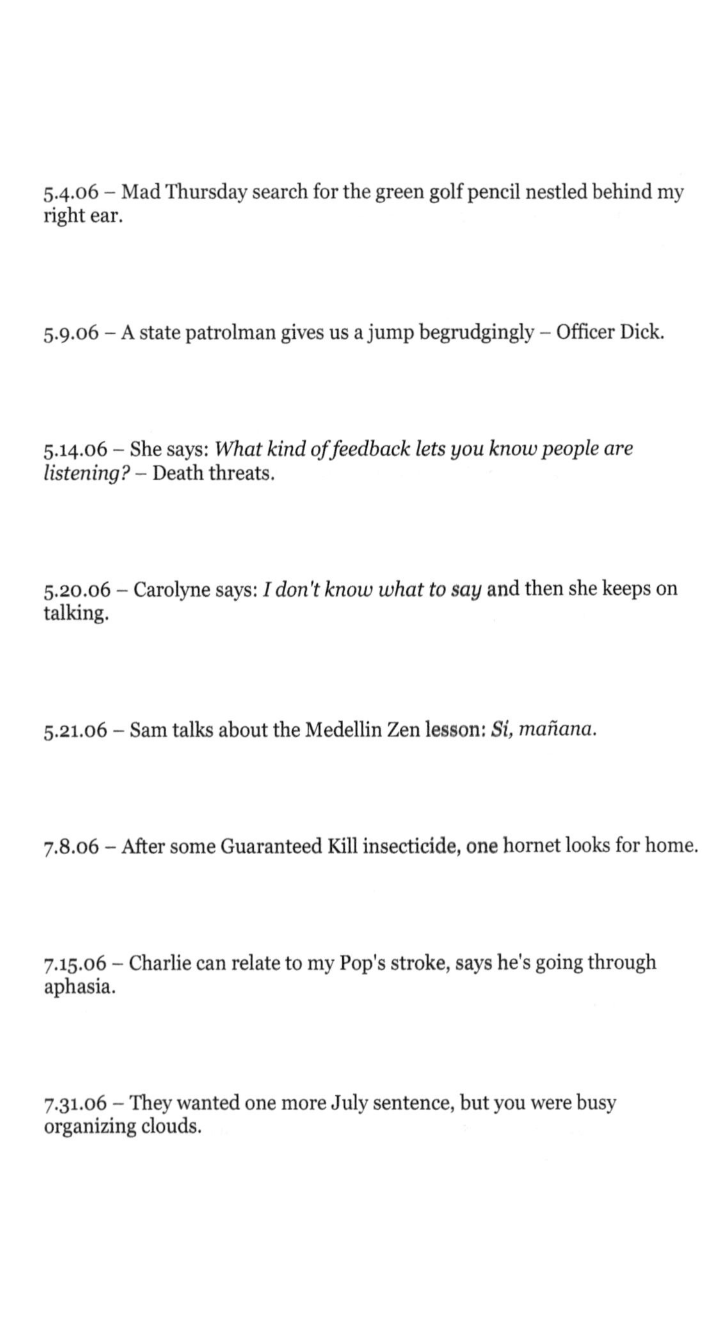

5.4.06 – Mad Thursday search for the green golf pencil nestled behind my right ear.

5.9.06 – A state patrolman gives us a jump begrudgingly – Officer Dick.

5.14.06 – She says: *What kind of feedback lets you know people are listening?* – Death threats.

5.20.06 – Carolyne says: *I don't know what to say* and then she keeps on talking.

5.21.06 – Sam talks about the Medellin Zen lesson: *Si, mañana.*

7.8.06 – After some Guaranteed Kill insecticide, one hornet looks for home.

7.15.06 – Charlie can relate to my Pop's stroke, says he's going through aphasia.

7.31.06 – They wanted one more July sentence, but you were busy organizing clouds.

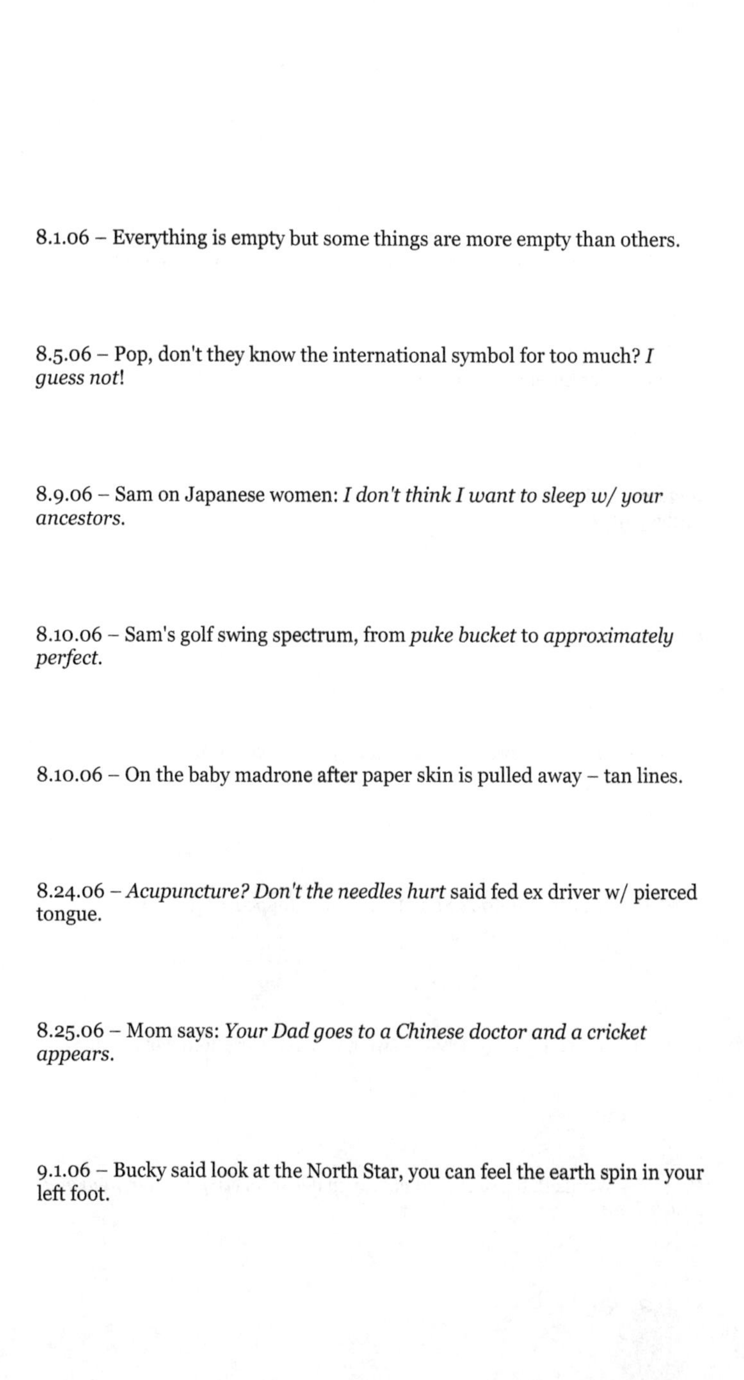

8.1.06 – Everything is empty but some things are more empty than others.

8.5.06 – Pop, don't they know the international symbol for too much? *I guess not*!

8.9.06 – Sam on Japanese women: *I don't think I want to sleep w/ your ancestors.*

8.10.06 – Sam's golf swing spectrum, from *puke bucket* to *approximately perfect.*

8.10.06 – On the baby madrone after paper skin is pulled away – tan lines.

8.24.06 – *Acupuncture? Don't the needles hurt* said fed ex driver w/ pierced tongue.

8.25.06 – Mom says: *Your Dad goes to a Chinese doctor and a cricket appears.*

9.1.06 – Bucky said look at the North Star, you can feel the earth spin in your left foot.

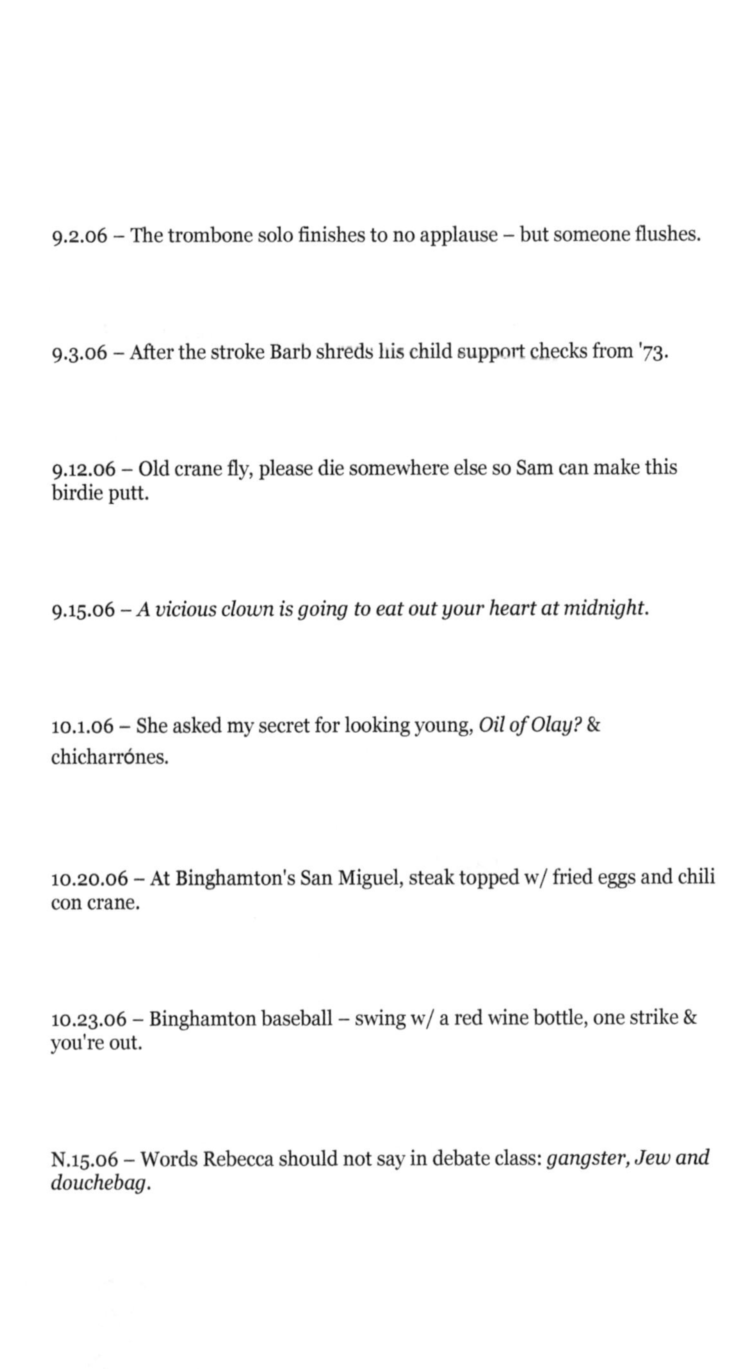

9.2.06 – The trombone solo finishes to no applause – but someone flushes.

9.3.06 – After the stroke Barb shreds his child support checks from '73.

9.12.06 – Old crane fly, please die somewhere else so Sam can make this birdie putt.

9.15.06 – *A vicious clown is going to eat out your heart at midnight.*

10.1.06 – She asked my secret for looking young, *Oil of Olay?* & chicharrónes.

10.20.06 – At Binghamton's San Miguel, steak topped w/ fried eggs and chili con crane.

10.23.06 – Binghamton baseball – swing w/ a red wine bottle, one strike & you're out.

N.15.06 – Words Rebecca should not say in debate class: *gangster, Jew and douchebag.*

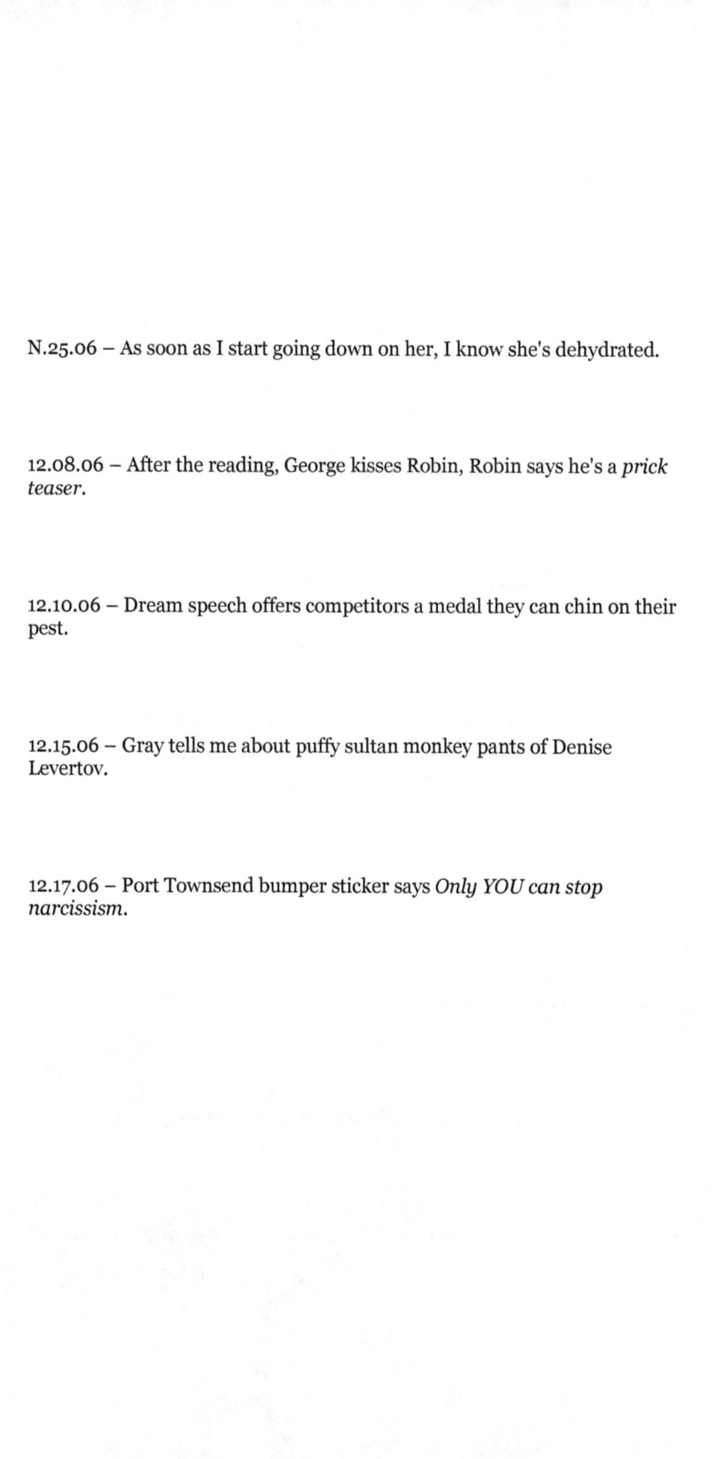

N.25.06 – As soon as I start going down on her, I know she's dehydrated.

12.08.06 – After the reading, George kisses Robin, Robin says he's a *prick teaser.*

12.10.06 – Dream speech offers competitors a medal they can chin on their pest.

12.15.06 – Gray tells me about puffy sultan monkey pants of Denise Levertov.

12.17.06 – Port Townsend bumper sticker says *Only YOU can stop narcissism.*

2007

1.19.07 – Get it in your mouth, not sure if you should swallow or not – oyster.

1.24.07 – The look on RR's dream face when the army crushes a piano.

1.25.07 – David fantasizing: *I wonder what she looks like without her cellphone.*

1.28.07 – Jeff, back from Massachusetts where he avoided the Sandwich Police.

2.9.07 – Steve's Civil Service motto: *Why work for an asshole when you can be one?*

2.18.07 – No one found Vincenzo dead in front of blaring TV for a year.

2.19.07 – I'm fixated on my spiritual quest when not torturing the cat.

3.8.07 – Rebecca says *I was drinking green tea before any of you Crackers.*

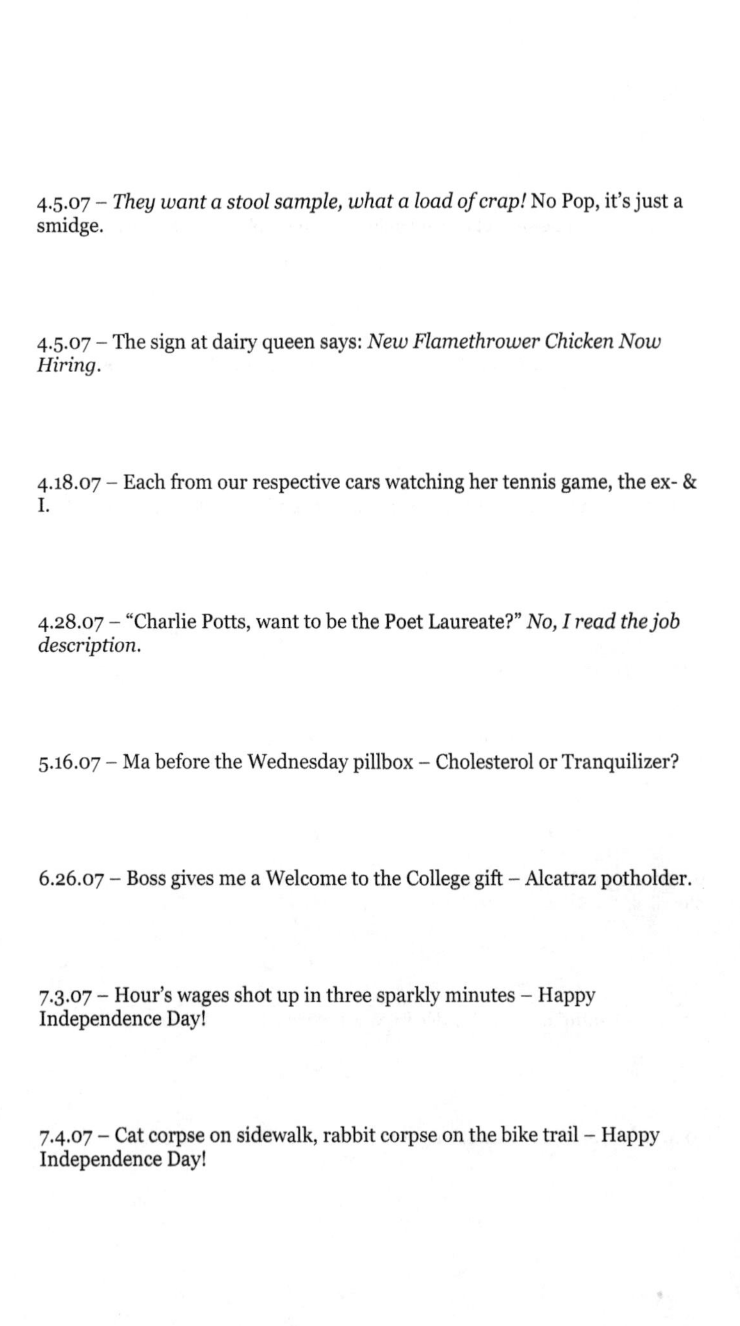

4.5.07 – *They want a stool sample, what a load of crap!* No Pop, it's just a smidge.

4.5.07 – The sign at dairy queen says: *New Flamethrower Chicken Now Hiring.*

4.18.07 – Each from our respective cars watching her tennis game, the ex- & I.

4.28.07 – "Charlie Potts, want to be the Poet Laureate?" *No, I read the job description.*

5.16.07 – Ma before the Wednesday pillbox – Cholesterol or Tranquilizer?

6.26.07 – Boss gives me a Welcome to the College gift – Alcatraz potholder.

7.3.07 – Hour's wages shot up in three sparkly minutes – Happy Independence Day!

7.4.07 – Cat corpse on sidewalk, rabbit corpse on the bike trail – Happy Independence Day!

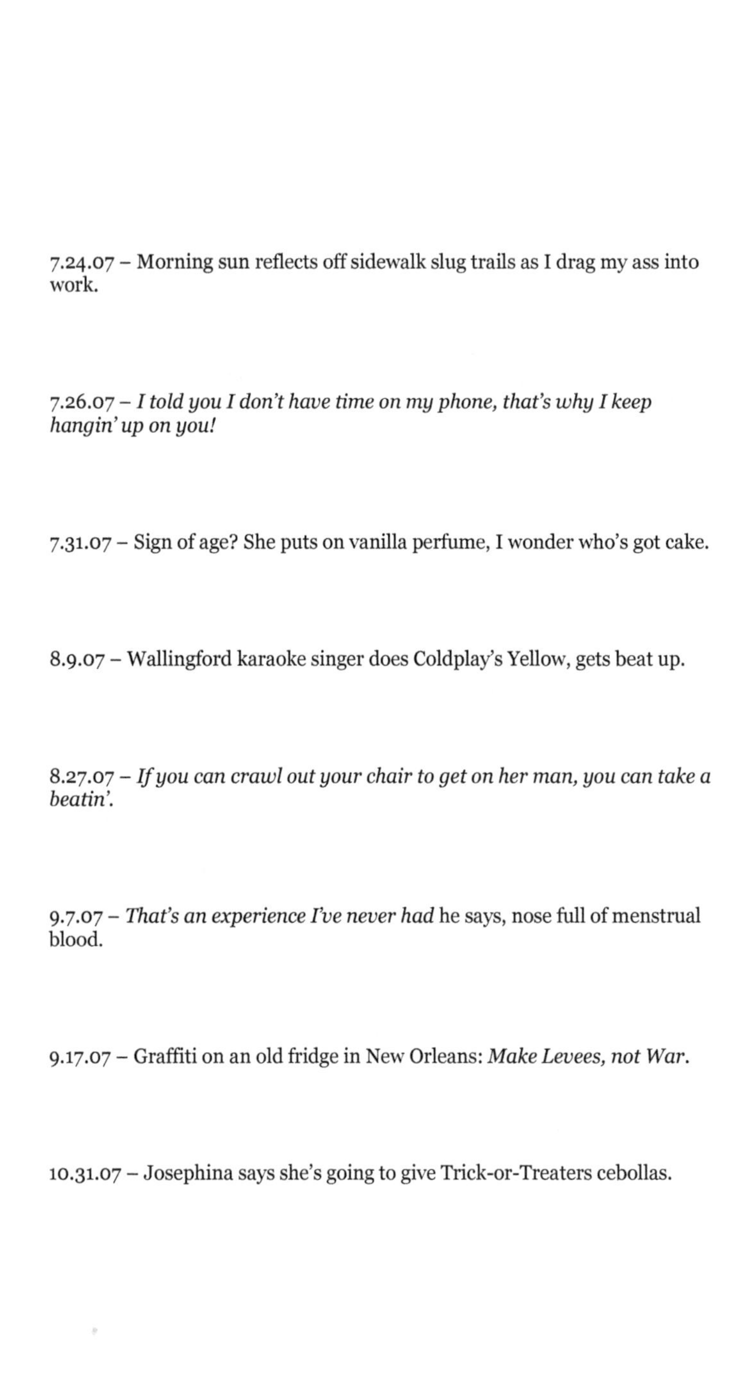

7.24.07 – Morning sun reflects off sidewalk slug trails as I drag my ass into work.

7.26.07 – *I told you I don't have time on my phone, that's why I keep hangin' up on you!*

7.31.07 – Sign of age? She puts on vanilla perfume, I wonder who's got cake.

8.9.07 – Wallingford karaoke singer does Coldplay's Yellow, gets beat up.

8.27.07 – *If you can crawl out your chair to get on her man, you can take a beatin'.*

9.7.07 – *That's an experience I've never had* he says, nose full of menstrual blood.

9.17.07 – Graffiti on an old fridge in New Orleans: *Make Levees, not War.*

10.31.07 – Josephina says she's going to give Trick-or-Treaters cebollas.

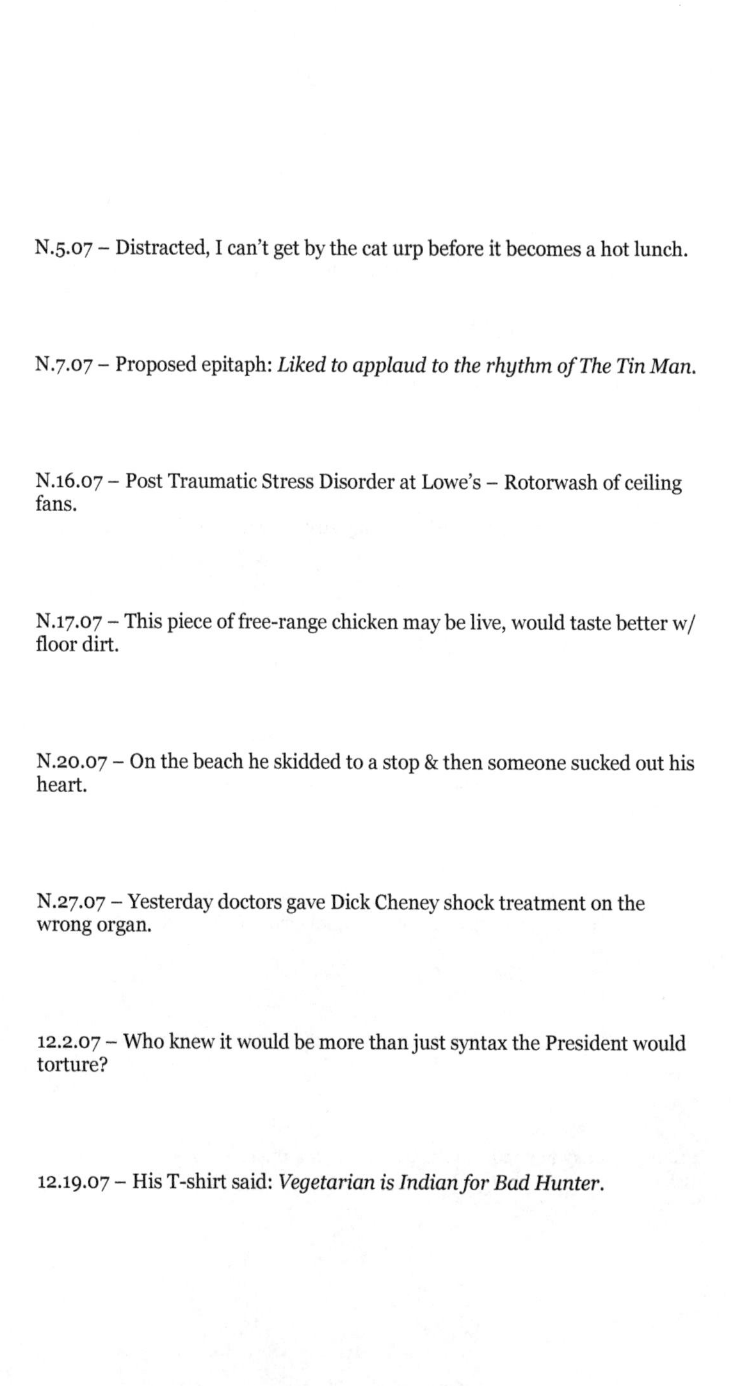

N.5.07 – Distracted, I can't get by the cat urp before it becomes a hot lunch.

N.7.07 – Proposed epitaph: *Liked to applaud to the rhythm of The Tin Man.*

N.16.07 – Post Traumatic Stress Disorder at Lowe's – Rotorwash of ceiling fans.

N.17.07 – This piece of free-range chicken may be live, would taste better w/ floor dirt.

N.20.07 – On the beach he skidded to a stop & then someone sucked out his heart.

N.27.07 – Yesterday doctors gave Dick Cheney shock treatment on the wrong organ.

12.2.07 – Who knew it would be more than just syntax the President would torture?

12.19.07 – His T-shirt said: *Vegetarian is Indian for Bad Hunter.*

2008

1.5.08 – Finish cleaning bathroom and toilet when another pubic hair falls.

1.17.08 – Oh no! Some of we starlings aren't going to make it across the river!

1.18.08 – They found the oldest surviving structure in California – dungeon.

1.18.08 – During his morning pill ritual, Pop's disgusted when I bring vitamins.

1.19.08 – Pop gives my chicken dinner high praise: *This tastes better than Amtrak.*

1.23.08 – If I could only ejaculate matcha, I'd have all my needs met.

2.15.08 – *The poet I.D.'s the circumstance in which the poem reveals itself.*

2.16.08 – Today Pop tells me: *I can't complain*, then he says the weather sucks.

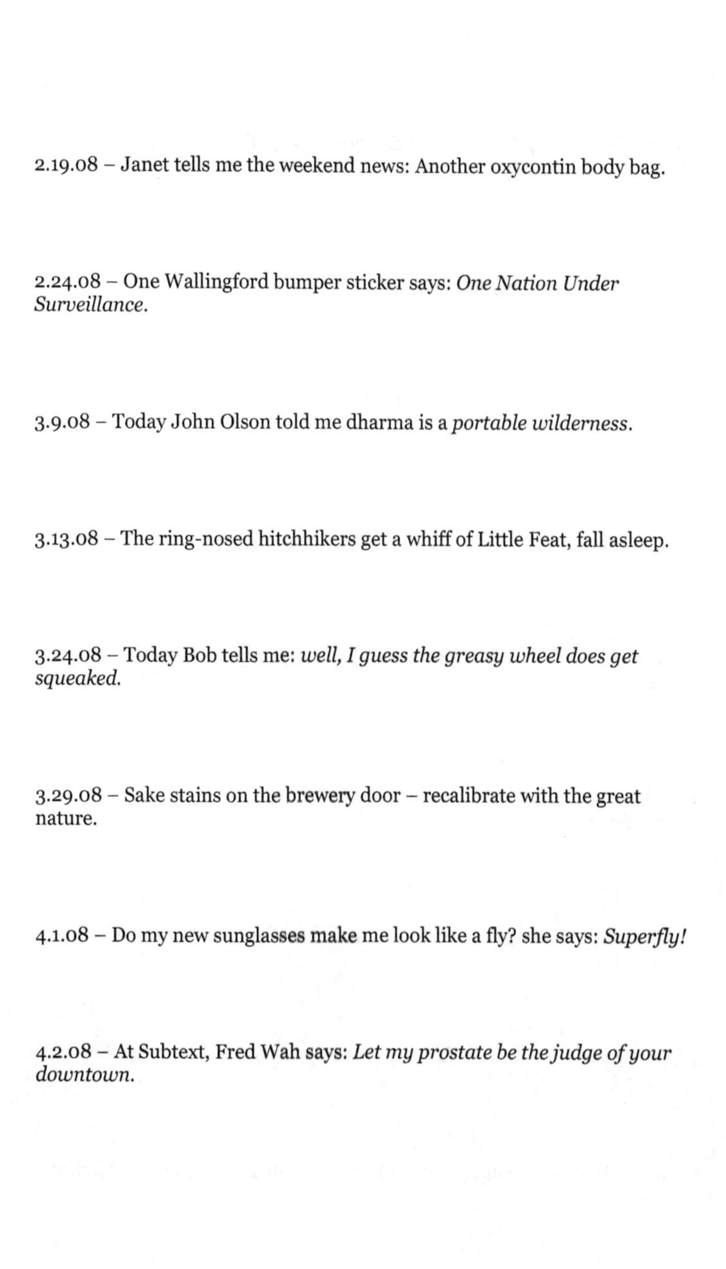

2.19.08 – Janet tells me the weekend news: Another oxycontin body bag.

2.24.08 – One Wallingford bumper sticker says: *One Nation Under Surveillance.*

3.9.08 – Today John Olson told me dharma is a *portable wilderness.*

3.13.08 – The ring-nosed hitchhikers get a whiff of Little Feat, fall asleep.

3.24.08 – Today Bob tells me: *well, I guess the greasy wheel does get squeaked.*

3.29.08 – Sake stains on the brewery door – recalibrate with the great nature.

4.1.08 – Do my new sunglasses make me look like a fly? she says: *Superfly!*

4.2.08 – At Subtext, Fred Wah says: *Let my prostate be the judge of your downtown.*

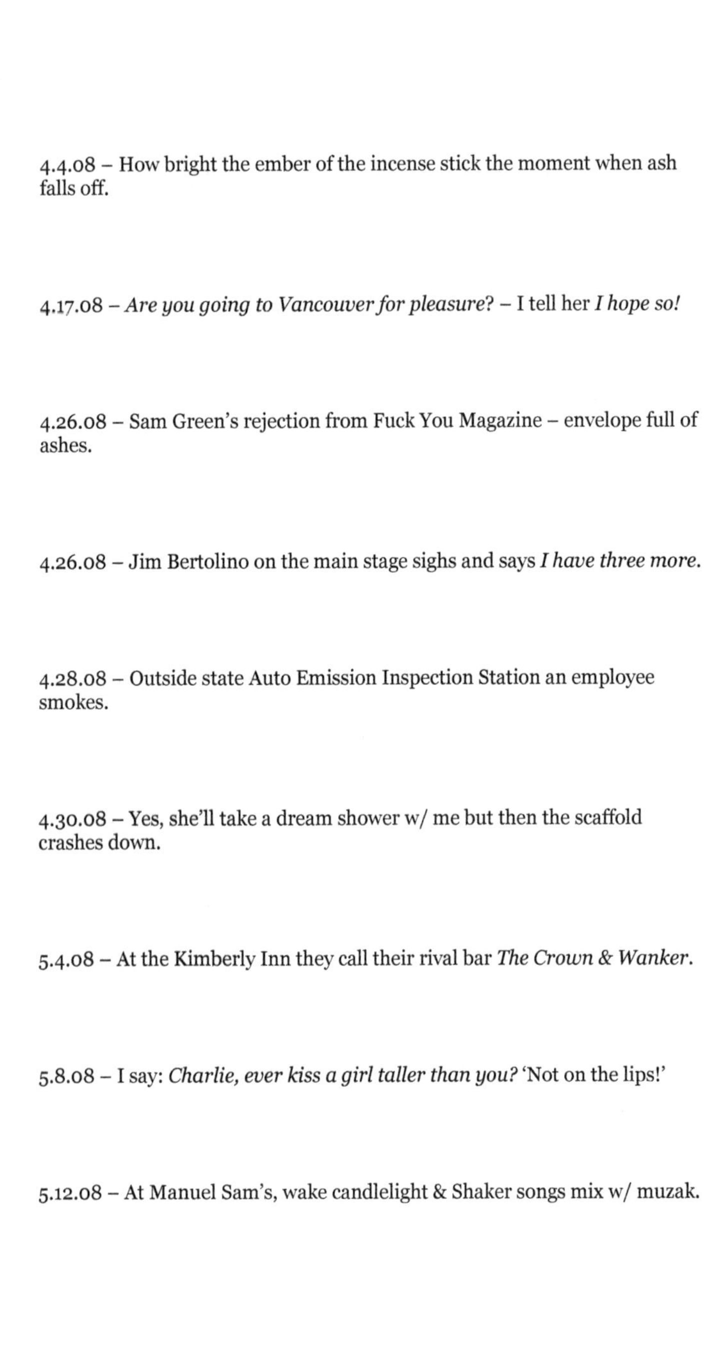

4.4.08 – How bright the ember of the incense stick the moment when ash falls off.

4.17.08 – *Are you going to Vancouver for pleasure*? – I tell her *I hope so!*

4.26.08 – Sam Green's rejection from Fuck You Magazine – envelope full of ashes.

4.26.08 – Jim Bertolino on the main stage sighs and says *I have three more.*

4.28.08 – Outside state Auto Emission Inspection Station an employee smokes.

4.30.08 – Yes, she'll take a dream shower w/ me but then the scaffold crashes down.

5.4.08 – At the Kimberly Inn they call their rival bar *The Crown & Wanker*.

5.8.08 – I say: *Charlie, ever kiss a girl taller than you?* 'Not on the lips!'

5.12.08 – At Manuel Sam's, wake candlelight & Shaker songs mix w/ muzak.

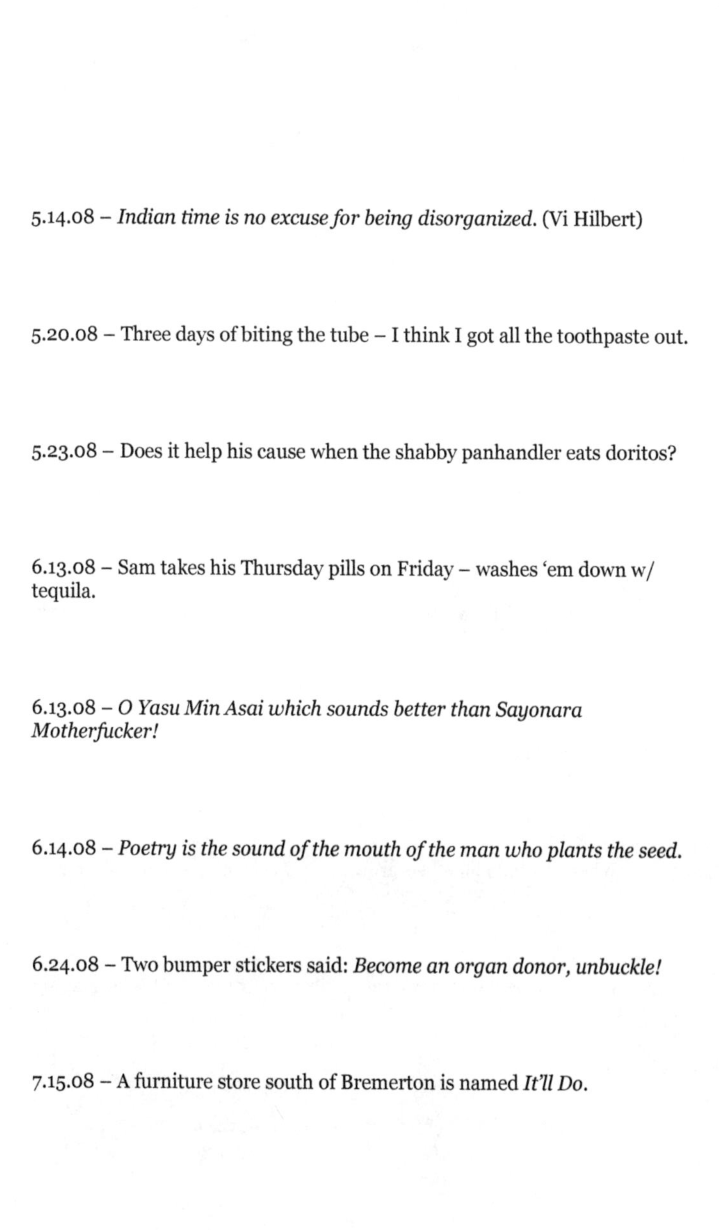

5.14.08 – *Indian time is no excuse for being disorganized.* (Vi Hilbert)

5.20.08 – Three days of biting the tube – I think I got all the toothpaste out.

5.23.08 – Does it help his cause when the shabby panhandler eats doritos?

6.13.08 – Sam takes his Thursday pills on Friday – washes ‘em down w/ tequila.

6.13.08 – *O Yasu Min Asai which sounds better than Sayonara Motherfucker!*

6.14.08 – *Poetry is the sound of the mouth of the man who plants the seed.*

6.24.08 – Two bumper stickers said: *Become an organ donor, unbuckle!*

7.15.08 – A furniture store south of Bremerton is named *It’ll Do.*

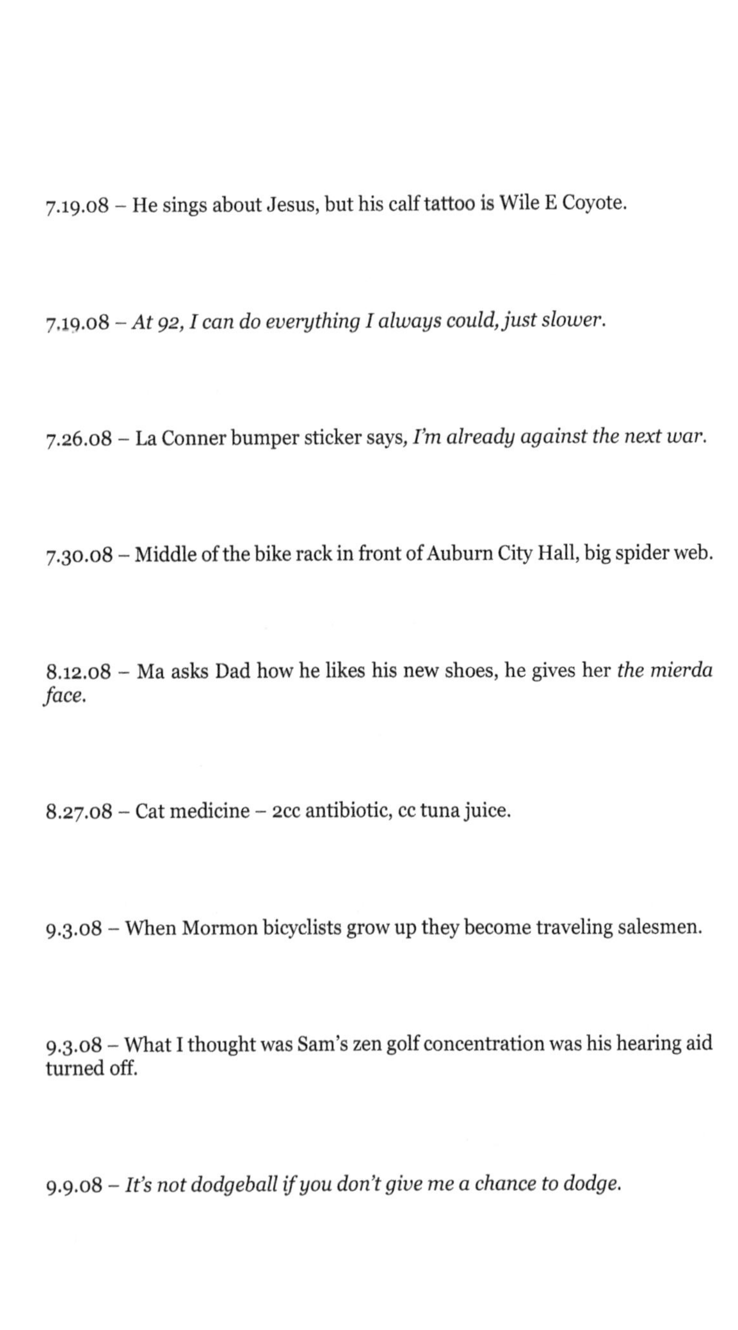

7.19.08 – He sings about Jesus, but his calf tattoo is Wile E Coyote.

7.19.08 – *At 92, I can do everything I always could, just slower.*

7.26.08 – La Conner bumper sticker says, *I'm already against the next war.*

7.30.08 – Middle of the bike rack in front of Auburn City Hall, big spider web.

8.12.08 – Ma asks Dad how he likes his new shoes, he gives her *the mierda face.*

8.27.08 – Cat medicine – 2cc antibiotic, cc tuna juice.

9.3.08 – When Mormon bicyclists grow up they become traveling salesmen.

9.3.08 – What I thought was Sam's zen golf concentration was his hearing aid turned off.

9.9.08 – *It's not dodgeball if you don't give me a chance to dodge.*

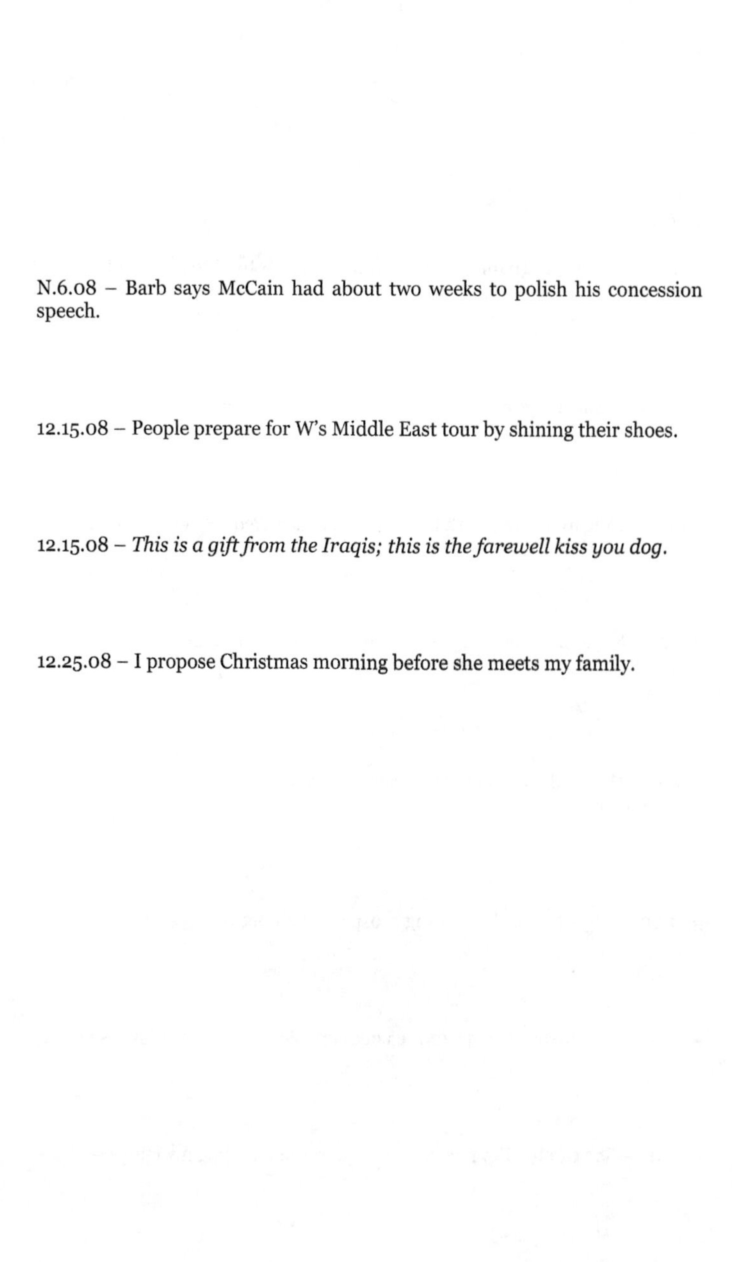

N.6.08 – Barb says McCain had about two weeks to polish his concession speech.

12.15.08 – People prepare for W's Middle East tour by shining their shoes.

12.15.08 – *This is a gift from the Iraqis; this is the farewell kiss you dog.*

12.25.08 – I propose Christmas morning before she meets my family.

2009

1.5.09 – Would her Thanksgiving stuffing been this hard to flush had we eaten it?

1.6.09 – Michael says he gets writer's block about 6 or 7 times a day.

3.1.09 – Tailgating @ 80 with his bumper sticker: *Real Men Love Jesus.*

3.4.09 – Something inside me wants to beat this cat until he learns to love me.

3.9.09 – Happy Birthday ex-wife – here's two tickets to Crime & Punishment.

3.17.09 – Augusto's on-line dating prospect, she's between 3 and 8 feet tall.

5.15.09 – She opens my copy erotic poem translations – an old lover's hair.

6.21.09 – She can tell I'm recovering – I've resumed biting my cuticles.

7.27.09 – Fat Grandpa Rutledge falls onto & kills the therapy Chihuahua.

9.9.09 – Elder couple leaves farmer's market, each holds a strap of paper shopping bag.

2010

1.23.10 – She'll wash cast-iron skillet only if she needs butter for popcorn.

1.25.10 – A bureaucrat's someone great finding reasons why they can not help you.

3.22.10 – Republican who yelled "Baby Killer" says comments were misconstrued.

3.29.10 – Are female suicide bombers greeted in heaven by virgins too?

4.23.10 – Seattle courtesy: truck driver waits as crows move chicken carcass.

4.26.10 – To a cat, jumping over your head during yoga – good idea.

4.28.10 – The sun in Seattle is a lot like a refrigerator light.

5.9.10 – Trying to keep raw eggs in the strike zone very hard in today's dream.

5.17.10 – *Plain blunt-ass mammal reason w/ the light of luminous intelligence.*

5.20.10 – In my next lifetime I'll rescue gym shoes hanging from telephone wires.

5.31.10 – Man inadvertently shoots himself in the testicles – "an accidental discharge."

6.19.10 – Eleven year old Hank says *I hate it when drag queens don't even try!*

6.19.10 – Hank's flick review: *Avatar is just Pocahontas with blue people!*

6.20.10 – Seattle solstice: Chihuahua shivers in cold rain outside starbucks.

7.1.10 – Sara says dying her hair makes her look younger – Ma says *From the scalp up!*

7.13.10 – From beyond the grave she sends me a social networking request.

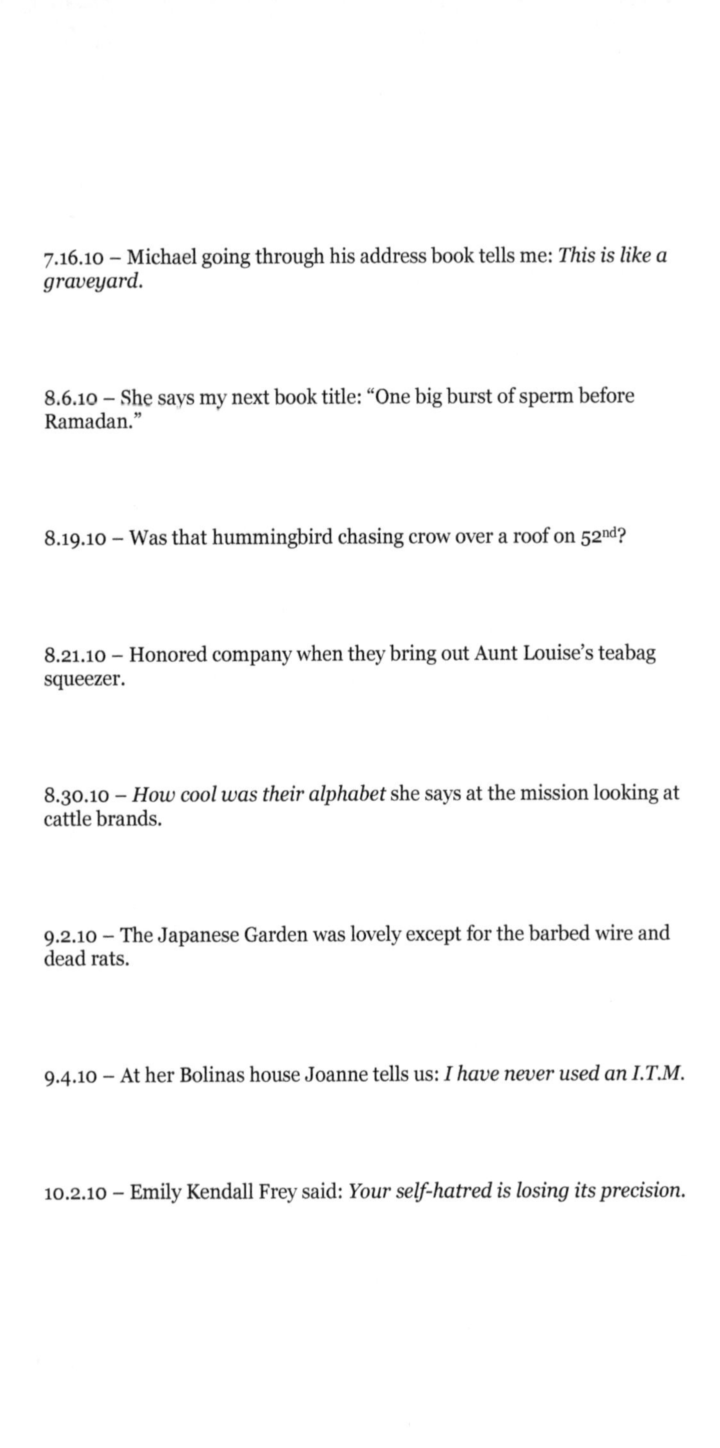

7.16.10 – Michael going through his address book tells me: *This is like a graveyard.*

8.6.10 – She says my next book title: “One big burst of sperm before Ramadan.”

8.19.10 – Was that hummingbird chasing crow over a roof on 52nd?

8.21.10 – Honored company when they bring out Aunt Louise’s teabag squeezer.

8.30.10 – *How cool was their alphabet* she says at the mission looking at cattle brands.

9.2.10 – The Japanese Garden was lovely except for the barbed wire and dead rats.

9.4.10 – At her Bolinas house Joanne tells us: *I have never used an I.T.M.*

10.2.10 – Emily Kendall Frey said: *Your self-hatred is losing its precision.*

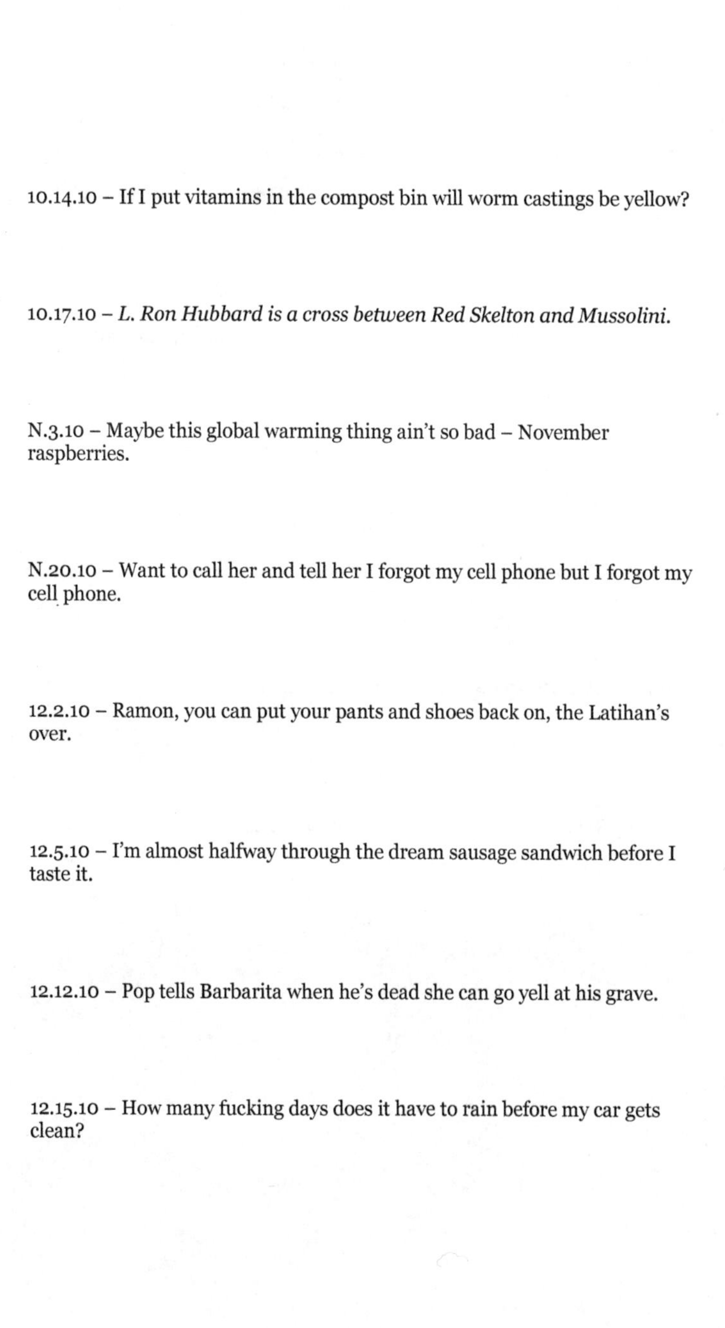

10.14.10 – If I put vitamins in the compost bin will worm castings be yellow?

10.17.10 – *L. Ron Hubbard is a cross between Red Skelton and Mussolini.*

N.3.10 – Maybe this global warming thing ain't so bad – November raspberries.

N.20.10 – Want to call her and tell her I forgot my cell phone but I forgot my cell phone.

12.2.10 – Ramon, you can put your pants and shoes back on, the Latihan's over.

12.5.10 – I'm almost halfway through the dream sausage sandwich before I taste it.

12.12.10 – Pop tells Barbarita when he's dead she can go yell at his grave.

12.15.10 – How many fucking days does it have to rain before my car gets clean?

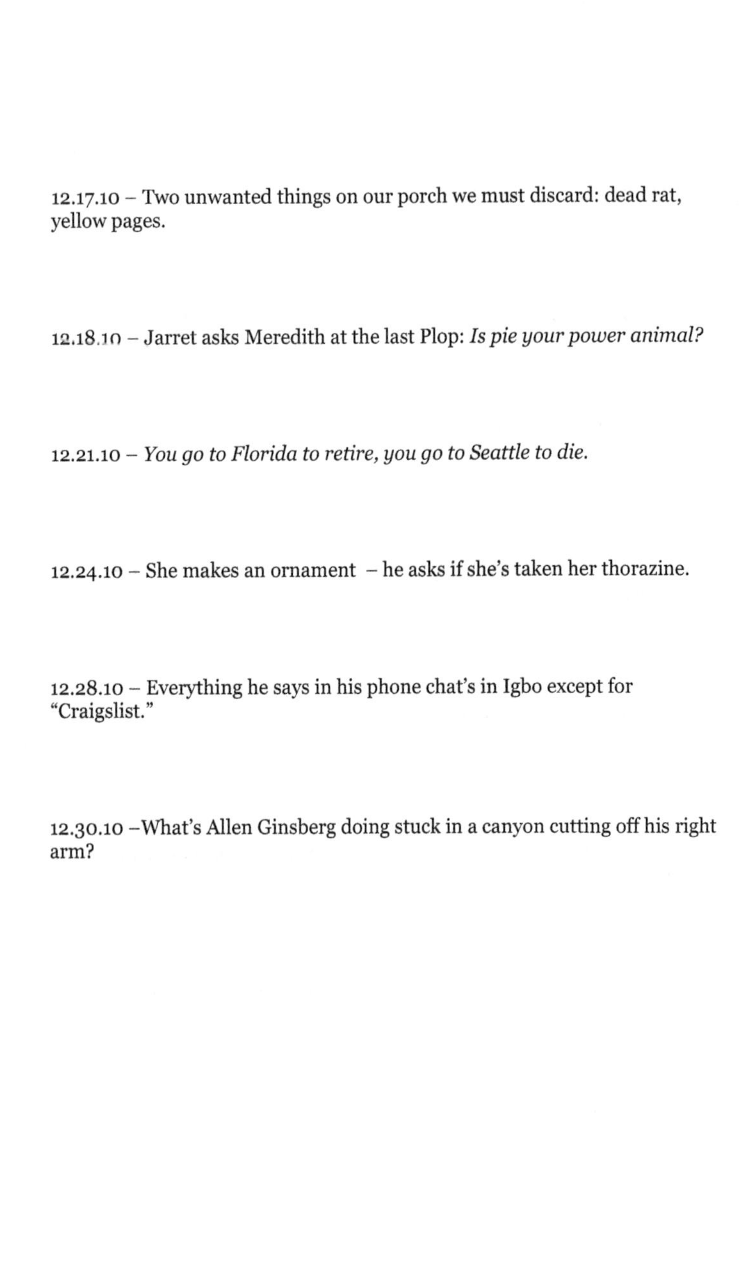

12.17.10 – Two unwanted things on our porch we must discard: dead rat, yellow pages.

12.18.10 – Jarret asks Meredith at the last Plop: *Is pie your power animal?*

12.21.10 – *You go to Florida to retire, you go to Seattle to die.*

12.24.10 – She makes an ornament – he asks if she's taken her thorazine.

12.28.10 – Everything he says in his phone chat's in Igbo except for "Craigslist."

12.30.10 –What's Allen Ginsberg doing stuck in a canyon cutting off his right arm?

2011

1.12.11 – Just because he has a bald spot doesn't mean he can't have a Mohawk.

2.10.11 – *He apparently only gets off the couch to eat grass & lick his ass.*

2.27.11 – I don't remember what year it was Pop stopped smiling in photographs.

3.6.11 – Poor little blood orange – I peel it only to find it's albino.

3.14.11 – With certain constellations the light takes so long to get here.

3.26.11 – Memorial balloons stuck in the branches of his family tree.

4.7.11 – Psoas – "the interface between security and identity."

5.1.11 – My students tell me, "Nobody but chance intervenes and saves the day."

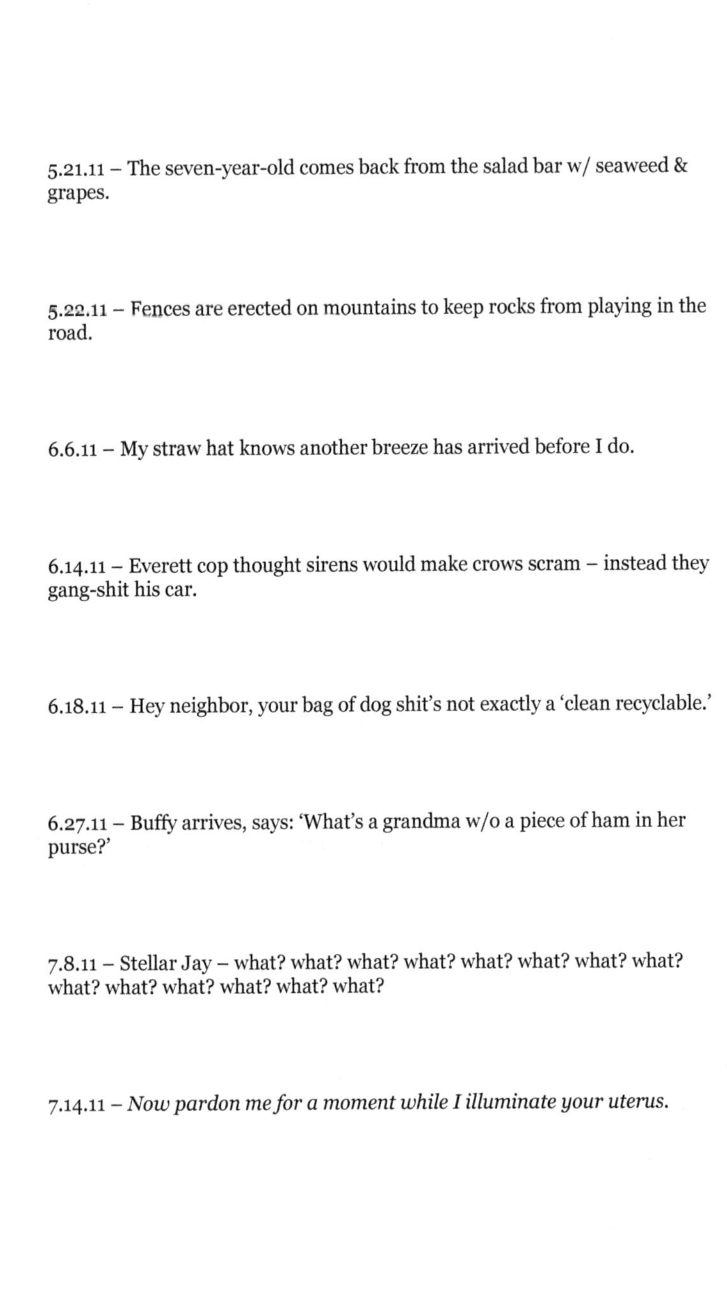

5.21.11 – The seven-year-old comes back from the salad bar w/ seaweed & grapes.

5.22.11 – Fences are erected on mountains to keep rocks from playing in the road.

6.6.11 – My straw hat knows another breeze has arrived before I do.

6.14.11 – Everett cop thought sirens would make crows scram – instead they gang-shit his car.

6.18.11 – Hey neighbor, your bag of dog shit's not exactly a 'clean recyclable.'

6.27.11 – Buffy arrives, says: 'What's a grandma w/o a piece of ham in her purse?'

7.8.11 – Stellar Jay – what? what? what? what? what? what? what? what? what? what? what? what? what? what?

7.14.11 – *Now pardon me for a moment while I illuminate your uterus.*

7.30.11 – You remember that hundred year flood we had a few years back? “Which one?”

8.6.11 – Pasta sold at SeaTac Airport, shaped like the needle called Space Noodles.

China Trip

8.7.11 – The Swedish poet has a breakfast of coffee and watermelon.

8.7.11 – Are you carrying any items on the dangerous good chart?

8.8.11 – At the banquet he said: It’s the best cow stomach salad I’ve ever had.

8.15.11 – The Xining vendor tells us the popsicle is “popsicle-flavored.”

8.15.11 – Tibetan herding his goats down the road w/ motorcycle & switch.

8.17.11 – The Thunderbolt of the wheel of time can’t stop traveler’s diarrhea.

8.23.11 – High up on the Great Wall above the buzz of cicadas – his phone rings.

8.27.11 – Our China motto: “Leave no Tibetan prayer wheel unturned.”

9.5.11 – At the home of Buster the three-legged cat, they offer gluten-free beer.

10.7.11 – I put down my cellphone as soon as I see the cop, but I’m in starbucks.

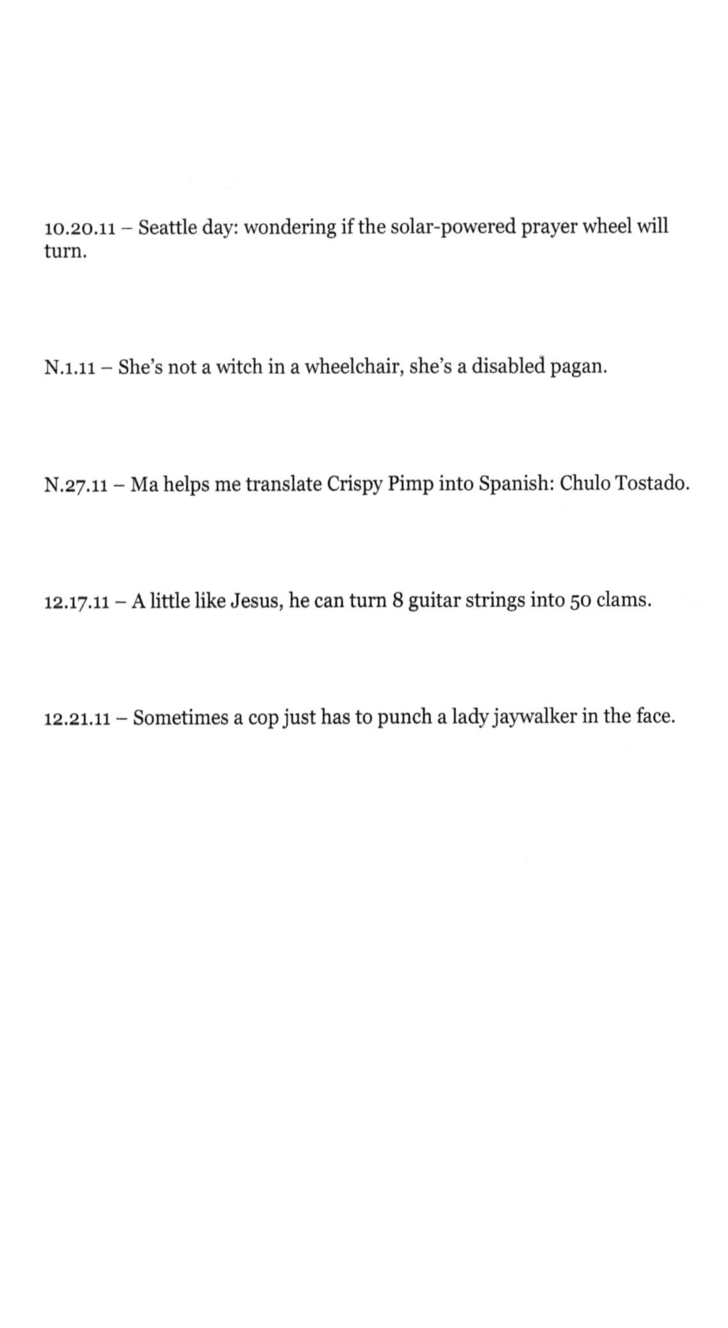

10.20.11 – Seattle day: wondering if the solar-powered prayer wheel will turn.

N.1.11 – She's not a witch in a wheelchair, she's a disabled pagan.

N.27.11 – Ma helps me translate Crispy Pimp into Spanish: Chulo Tostado.

12.17.11 – A little like Jesus, he can turn 8 guitar strings into 50 clams.

12.21.11 – Sometimes a cop just has to punch a lady jaywalker in the face.

2012

1.4.12 – Northwest Church memorial service: gluten free communion wafers.

1.6.12 – He has closed his car trunk at least 17 times since he last washed it.

1.9.12 – Xi Chuan says International District dragons look more like mountain lizards.

1.13.12 – Useless! Useless! – flossing in the mid-day, eating popcorn at night.

1.15.12 – *I'm open-minded but I get nervous when Christians get out guitars.*

1.29.12 – It only takes one fucker smoking to forever scar a blanket.

2.11.12 – Phrase I was not expecting to hear this morning: "Veins of the rectum."

2.25.12 – Hey Pocky Way, either: "You can't believe that" or "Kill the guy over there."

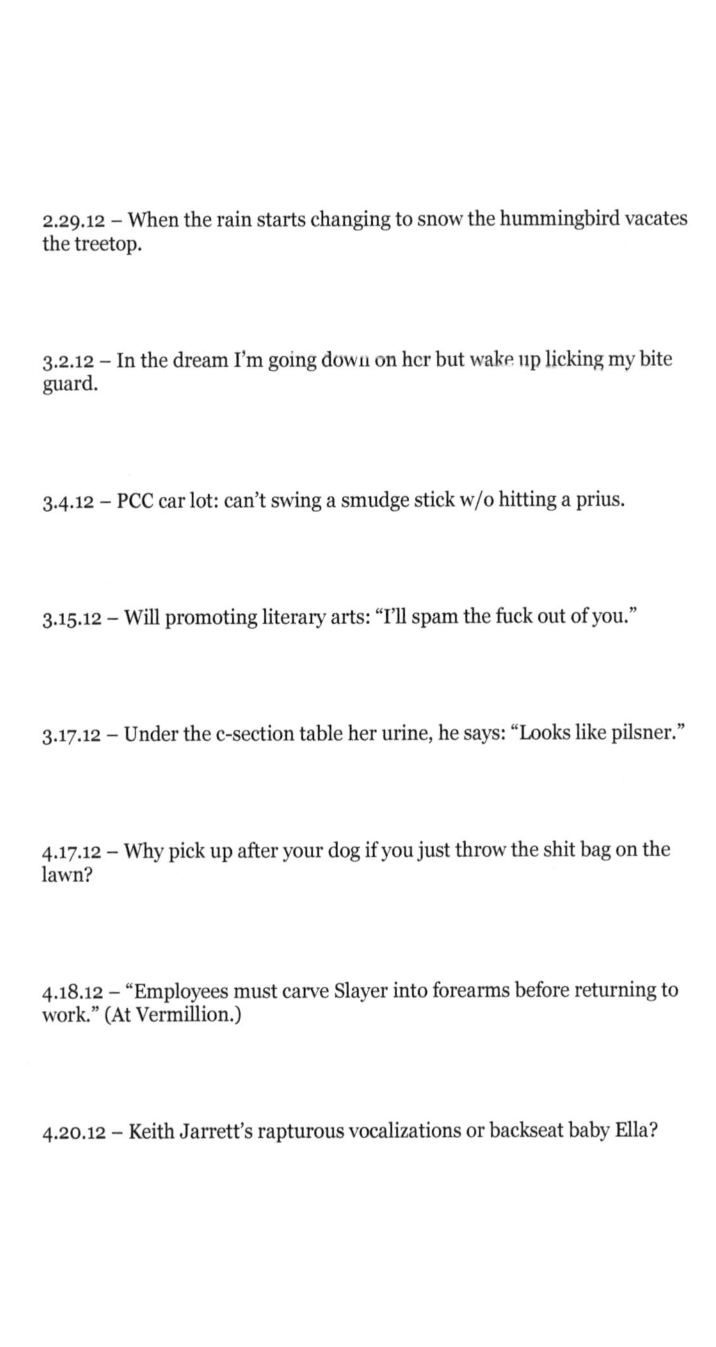

2.29.12 – When the rain starts changing to snow the hummingbird vacates the treetop.

3.2.12 – In the dream I'm going down on her but wake up licking my bite guard.

3.4.12 – PCC car lot: can't swing a smudge stick w/o hitting a prius.

3.15.12 – Will promoting literary arts: "I'll spam the fuck out of you."

3.17.12 – Under the c-section table her urine, he says: "Looks like pilsner."

4.17.12 – Why pick up after your dog if you just throw the shit bag on the lawn?

4.18.12 – "Employees must carve Slayer into forearms before returning to work." (At Vermillion.)

4.20.12 – Keith Jarrett's rapturous vocalizations or backseat baby Ella?

4.29.12 – My head feels like a bear split it w/ his claw & shit in it.

5.6.12 – Pop talking about Santiago's screwball: *I guess it just didn't screw!*

5.20.12 – Translating Deviled Eggs into Spanish harder than "Huevos de Lucifer."

5.31.12 – Not unlike a fart he rolls down car window to let out bad music.

6.11.12 – One daughter drinks formula, one root beer floats w/ whipped cream-flavored vodka.

6.23.12 – Three days after the 2nd break-in, Dave is throwing rocks at squirrels.

6.27.12 – The next guy who asks: "Are you the Grandfather? – gets a cane in the shin.

6.29.12 – *Look Ma, no hands!* he texts on his cellphone while riding his bicycle.

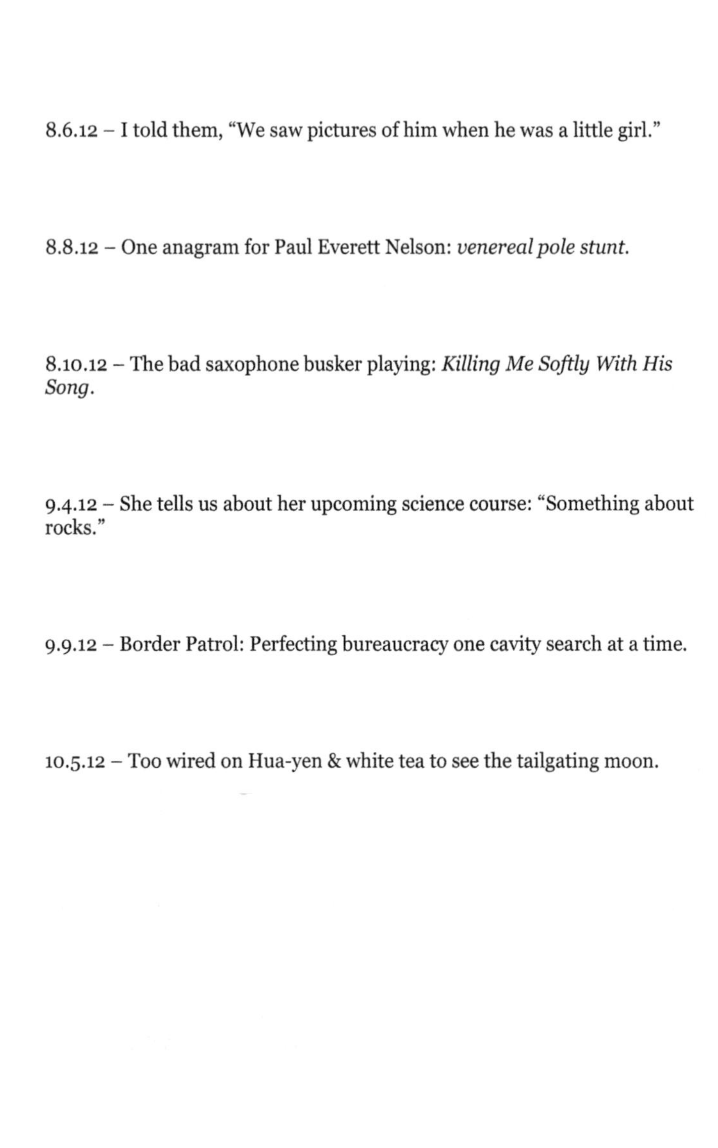

8.6.12 – I told them, “We saw pictures of him when he was a little girl.”

8.8.12 – One anagram for Paul Everett Nelson: *venereal pole stunt.*

8.10.12 – The bad saxophone busker playing: *Killing Me Softly With His Song*.

9.4.12 – She tells us about her upcoming science course: “Something about rocks.”

9.9.12 – Border Patrol: Perfecting bureaucracy one cavity search at a time.

10.5.12 – Too wired on Hua-yen & white tea to see the tailgating moon.

2013

1.15.13 – Eighteen human heads found at O'Hare Airport have nothing to declare.

1.20.13 – Only a white person would try to strangle someone with their dreadlocks.

2.19.13 – Bad idea to ask a guy with a hernia: "How's it hangin'?"

2.26.13 – The winter fly died trying to get inside the disposable diaper.

3.1.13 – Nurse Luz asks: "Do you have any body piercings? – "not that I know of."

3.14.13 – It's either applause once the jazz tune stops or rain hitting the windshield.

3.14.13 – w/ oxy, find I'm the age to prefer a good shit over a high.

3.21.13 – The after-lunch cookie was too much snicker and not enough doodle.

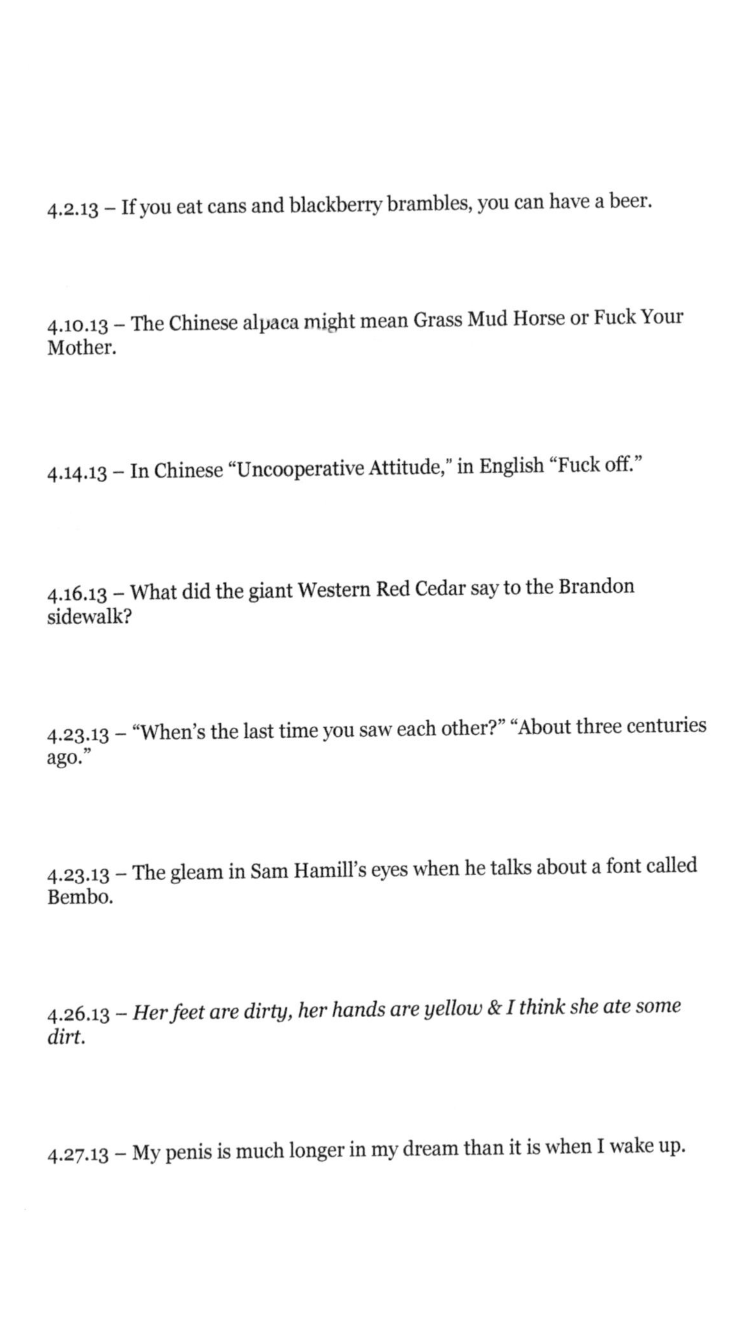

4.2.13 – If you eat cans and blackberry brambles, you can have a beer.

4.10.13 – The Chinese alpaca might mean Grass Mud Horse or Fuck Your Mother.

4.14.13 – In Chinese “Uncooperative Attitude,” in English “Fuck off.”

4.16.13 – What did the giant Western Red Cedar say to the Brandon sidewalk?

4.23.13 – “When’s the last time you saw each other?” “About three centuries ago.”

4.23.13 – The gleam in Sam Hamill’s eyes when he talks about a font called Bembo.

4.26.13 – *Her feet are dirty, her hands are yellow & I think she ate some dirt.*

4.27.13 – My penis is much longer in my dream than it is when I wake up.

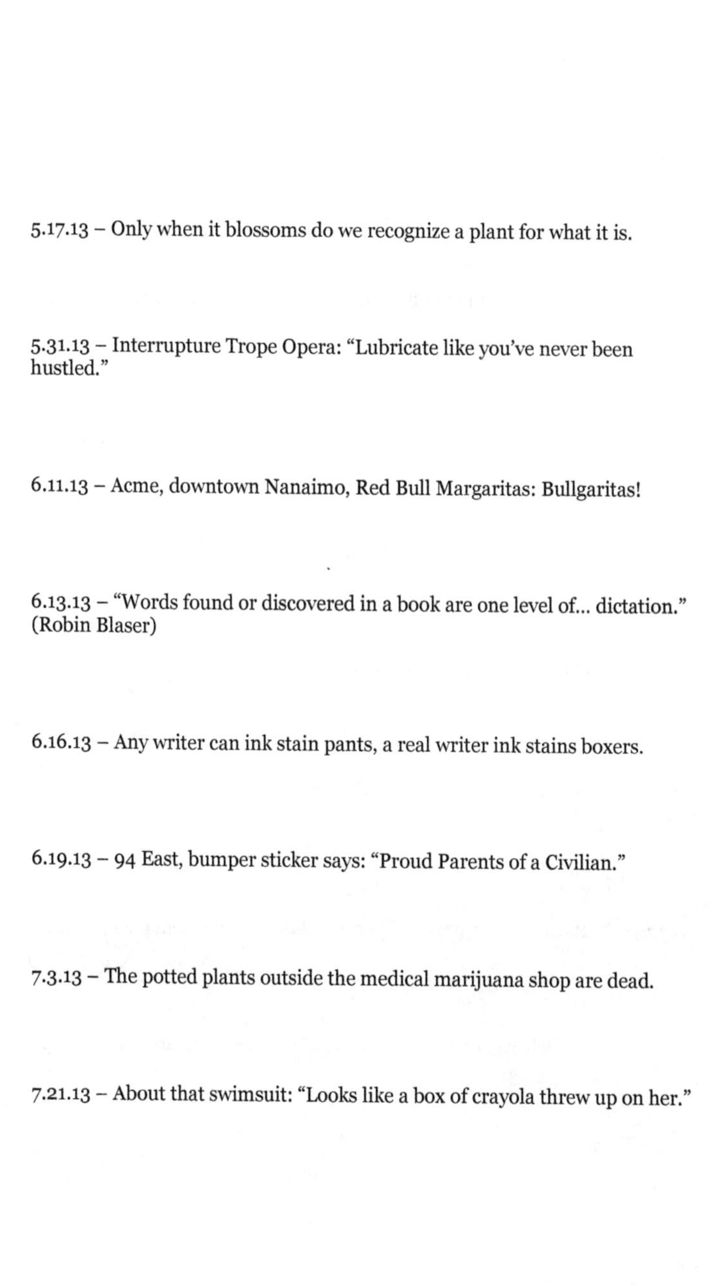

5.17.13 – Only when it blossoms do we recognize a plant for what it is.

5.31.13 – Interrupture Trope Opera: “Lubricate like you’ve never been hustled.”

6.11.13 – Acme, downtown Nanaimo, Red Bull Margaritas: Bullgaritas!

6.13.13 – “Words found or discovered in a book are one level of... dictation.” (Robin Blaser)

6.16.13 – Any writer can ink stain pants, a real writer ink stains boxers.

6.19.13 – 94 East, bumper sticker says: “Proud Parents of a Civilian.”

7.3.13 – The potted plants outside the medical marijuana shop are dead.

7.21.13 – About that swimsuit: “Looks like a box of crayola threw up on her.”

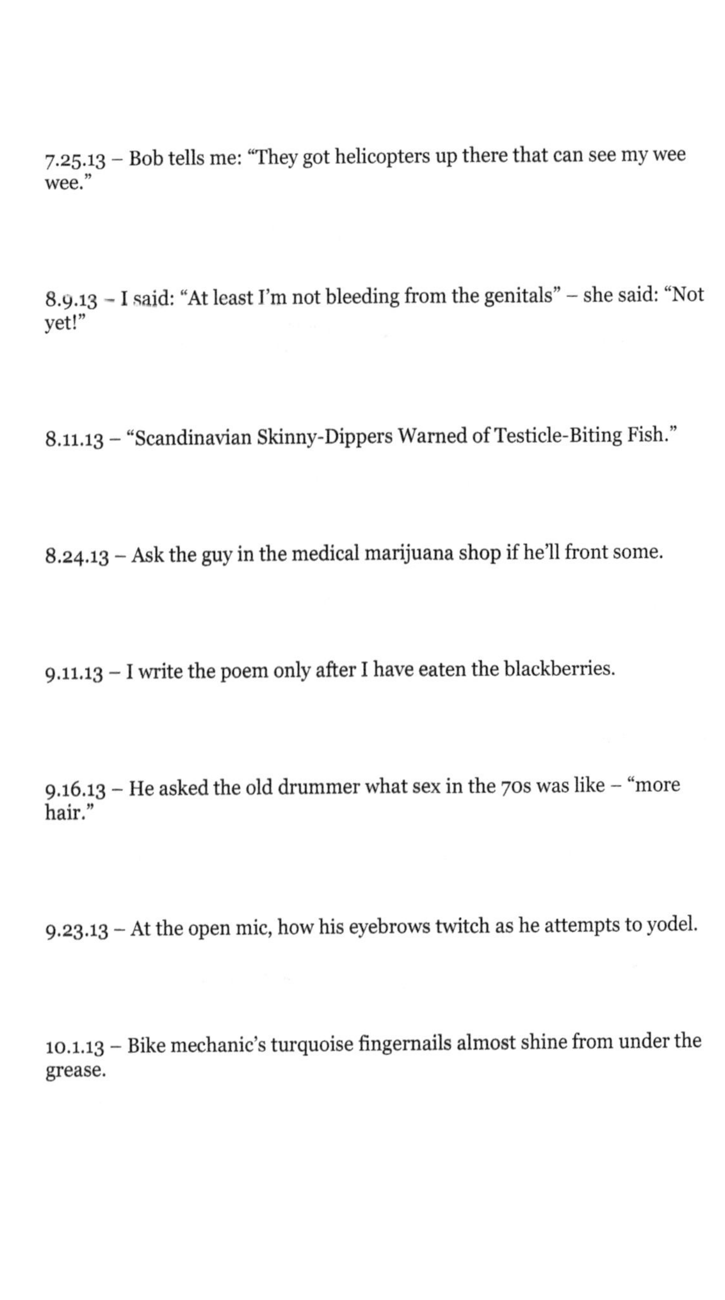

7.25.13 – Bob tells me: “They got helicopters up there that can see my wee wee.”

8.9.13 – I said: “At least I’m not bleeding from the genitals” – she said: “Not yet!”

8.11.13 – “Scandinavian Skinny-Dippers Warned of Testicle-Biting Fish.”

8.24.13 – Ask the guy in the medical marijuana shop if he’ll front some.

9.11.13 – I write the poem only after I have eaten the blackberries.

9.16.13 – He asked the old drummer what sex in the 70s was like – “more hair.”

9.23.13 – At the open mic, how his eyebrows twitch as he attempts to yodel.

10.1.13 – Bike mechanic’s turquoise fingernails almost shine from under the grease.

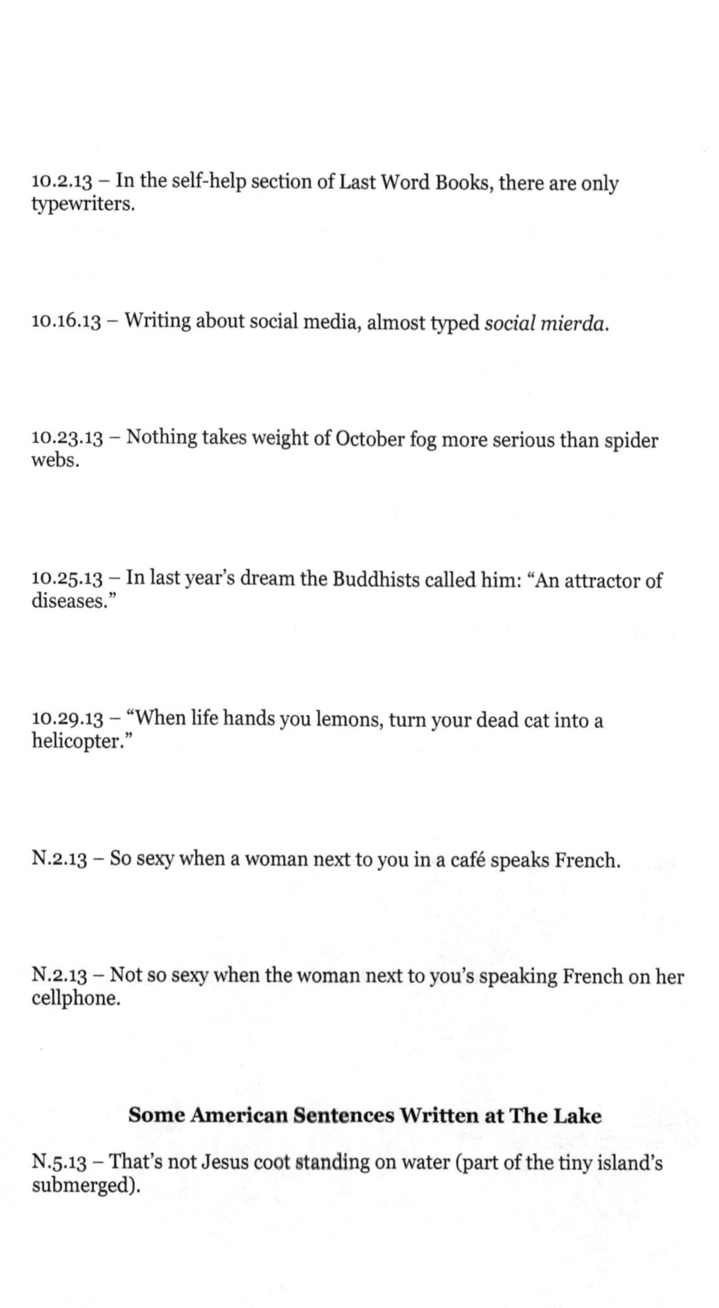

10.2.13 – In the self-help section of Last Word Books, there are only typewriters.

10.16.13 – Writing about social media, almost typed *social mierda.*

10.23.13 – Nothing takes weight of October fog more serious than spider webs.

10.25.13 – In last year's dream the Buddhists called him: "An attractor of diseases."

10.29.13 – "When life hands you lemons, turn your dead cat into a helicopter."

N.2.13 – So sexy when a woman next to you in a café speaks French.

N.2.13 – Not so sexy when the woman next to you's speaking French on her cellphone.

Some American Sentences Written at The Lake

N.5.13 – That's not Jesus coot standing on water (part of the tiny island's submerged).

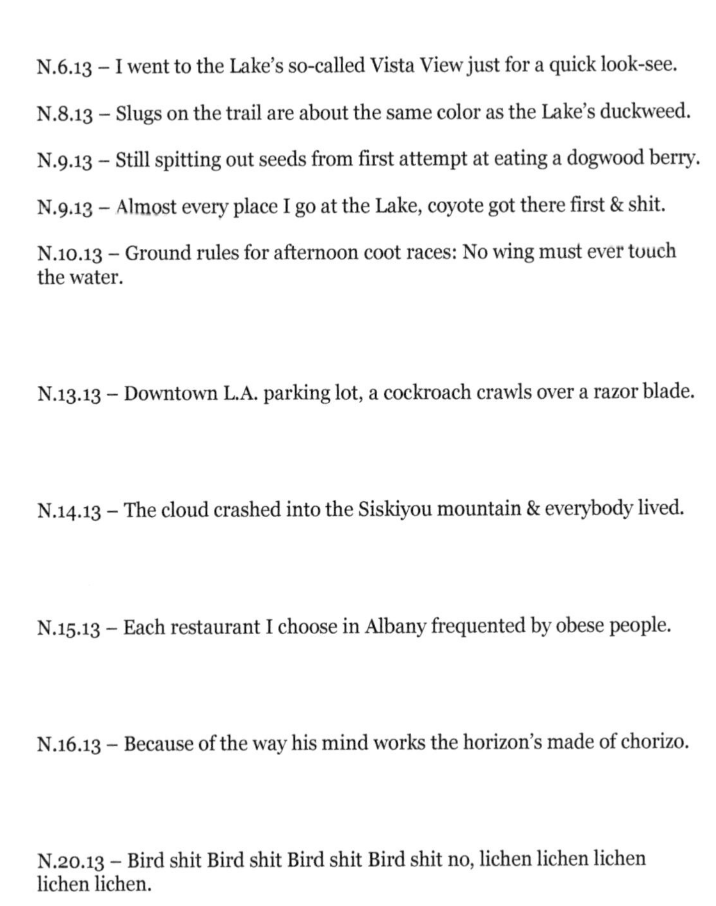

N.6.13 – I went to the Lake's so-called Vista View just for a quick look-see.

N.8.13 – Slugs on the trail are about the same color as the Lake's duckweed.

N.9.13 – Still spitting out seeds from first attempt at eating a dogwood berry.

N.9.13 – Almost every place I go at the Lake, coyote got there first & shit.

N.10.13 – Ground rules for afternoon coot races: No wing must ever touch the water.

N.13.13 – Downtown L.A. parking lot, a cockroach crawls over a razor blade.

N.14.13 – The cloud crashed into the Siskiyou mountain & everybody lived.

N.15.13 – Each restaurant I choose in Albany frequented by obese people.

N.16.13 – Because of the way his mind works the horizon's made of chorizo.

N.20.13 – Bird shit Bird shit Bird shit Bird shit no, lichen lichen lichen lichen lichen.

N.23.13 – Wanda Coleman indeed's been "seized and surrendered her terrible squawk."

2014

1.3.14 – A sort of Sudhana seeks the genius loci of Cascadia.

1.5.14 – Motherfucker Motherfucker Motherfucker Motherfucker Moth...

1.6.14 – Parent at the toddler gym can't do the hula hoop while she chews gum.

1.8.14 – Not clouds passing by the waxing moon, shadow of prayer flags by porch light.

1.16.14 – His tradition "points him to God" but he's headed for the salad bar.

1.20.14 – In ancient China Sam says he and I'd have been "scholars out of office."

1.22.14 – Facebook is over now so your children can accept your friend request.

1.23.14 – To an ESL class explain the phrase: "I've a lot of shit on my plate."

1.24.14 – Not a sidewalk shower head – one standing January sunflower.

1.29.14 – Every time I get a glimpse of that Shar Pei he has a confused look.

1.13.14 – He's got his hand so far up the bell of his French horn it hurts.

2.2.14 – How Seattle fans root in the Super Bowl: "Go Seahawks, Namaste."

2.4.14 – Not electricity zipping through the wires, chitter of bushtits.

2.8.14 – Lectured on what's "original" by the drummer of a cover band.

2.12.14 – Bank robbing in a dream – there's only so much cash you can stash in your socks.

2.14.14 – Better write down today's American Sentence before I get drunk.

2.23.14 – The moss-laden branches can only survive the snow storm for so long.

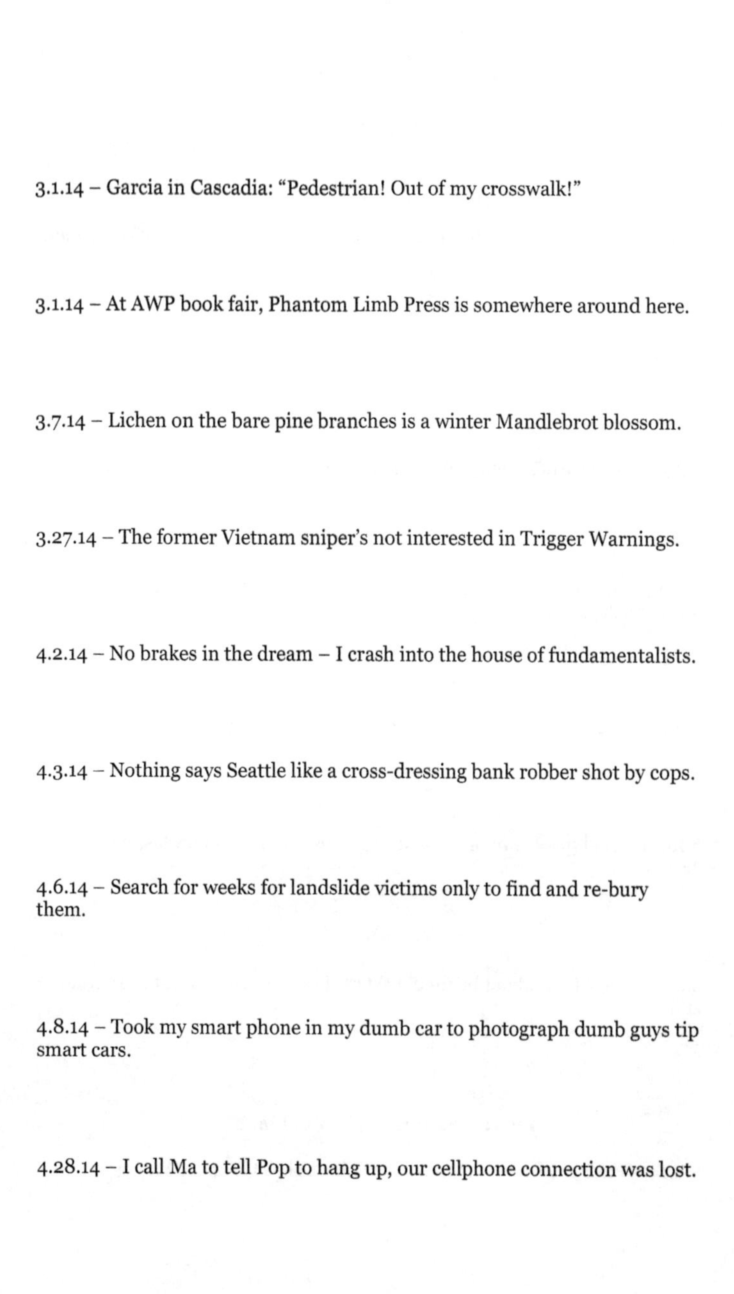

3.1.14 – Garcia in Cascadia: “Pedestrian! Out of my crosswalk!”

3.1.14 – At AWP book fair, Phantom Limb Press is somewhere around here.

3.7.14 – Lichen on the bare pine branches is a winter Mandlebrot blossom.

3.27.14 – The former Vietnam sniper’s not interested in Trigger Warnings.

4.2.14 – No brakes in the dream – I crash into the house of fundamentalists.

4.3.14 – Nothing says Seattle like a cross-dressing bank robber shot by cops.

4.6.14 – Search for weeks for landslide victims only to find and re-bury them.

4.8.14 – Took my smart phone in my dumb car to photograph dumb guys tip smart cars.

4.28.14 – I call Ma to tell Pop to hang up, our cellphone connection was lost.

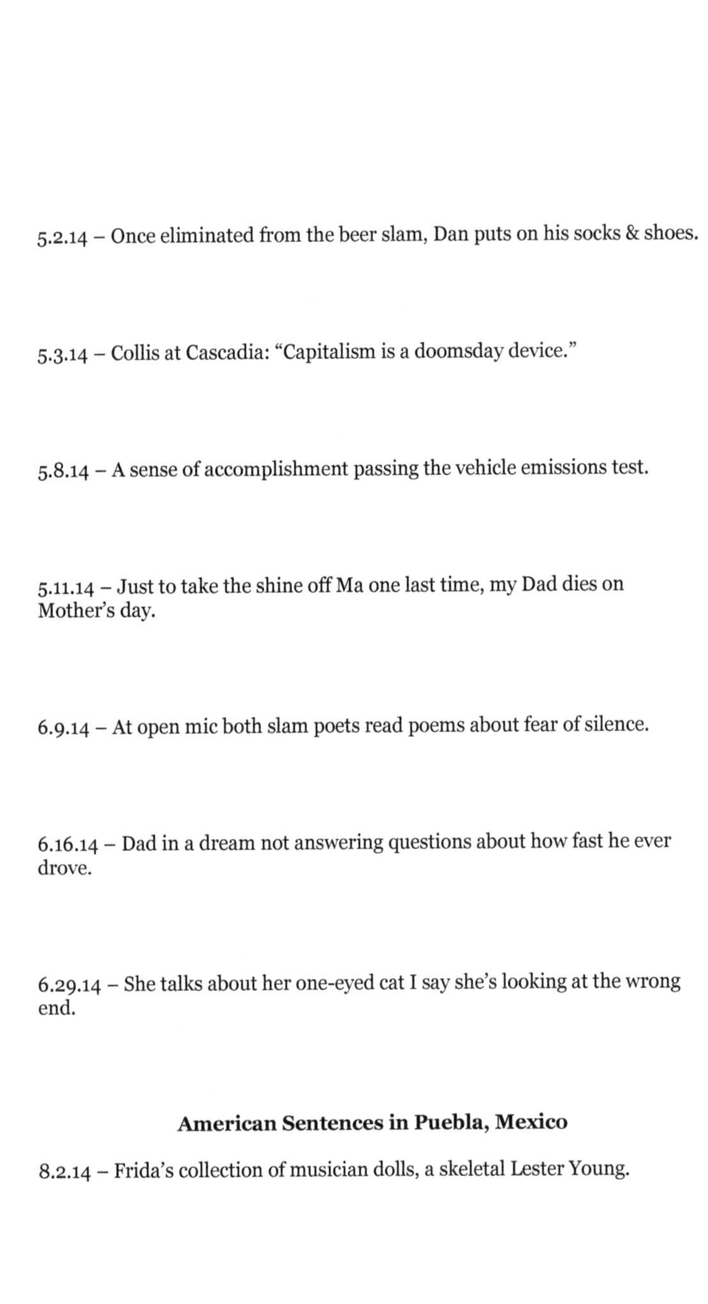

5.2.14 – Once eliminated from the beer slam, Dan puts on his socks & shoes.

5.3.14 – Collis at Cascadia: “Capitalism is a doomsday device.”

5.8.14 – A sense of accomplishment passing the vehicle emissions test.

5.11.14 – Just to take the shine off Ma one last time, my Dad dies on Mother’s day.

6.9.14 – At open mic both slam poets read poems about fear of silence.

6.16.14 – Dad in a dream not answering questions about how fast he ever drove.

6.29.14 – She talks about her one-eyed cat I say she’s looking at the wrong end.

American Sentences in Puebla, Mexico

8.2.14 – Frida’s collection of musician dolls, a skeletal Lester Young.

8.3.14 – "I'm Colombian by birth, Mexican at heart, my stomach is gringo." (Juan Felix)

8.3.14 – Cross a Pomeranian w/ a Chihuahua & get a Pomihuahua. (Melissa Brannon)

8.6.14 – Shop for sombreros, some beauties, but my American head's too big.

8.7.14 – Bapak: "I've given you rocket fuel & you use it like chicken shit."

8.7.14 – Only at a World Congress would a performer have a backup mime.

8.7.14 – Only at Subud would that backup mime become foundation chair.

8.8.14 – Not sure which toilet button to press after Montezuma's Revenge.

8.12.14 – Pablo feeding leftover chicarrones to the Puebla pigeons.

8.14.14 – Pablo Vargas Lugo knows how the flags of the butterfly nations fly.

8.16.14 – This Puebla bus driver in a previous life, a caballero.

8.23.14 – Dad would say while driving: "I've got two words for you and they ain't 'let's dance!'"

9.18.14 – Warne Marsh on Tristano: "Finally form itself could be improvised." (1945)

9.20.14 – I wanted to smash that fruit fly landed on Faiza's white hijab.

9.22.14 – Too early in the season for frozen vomit on the side of the car.

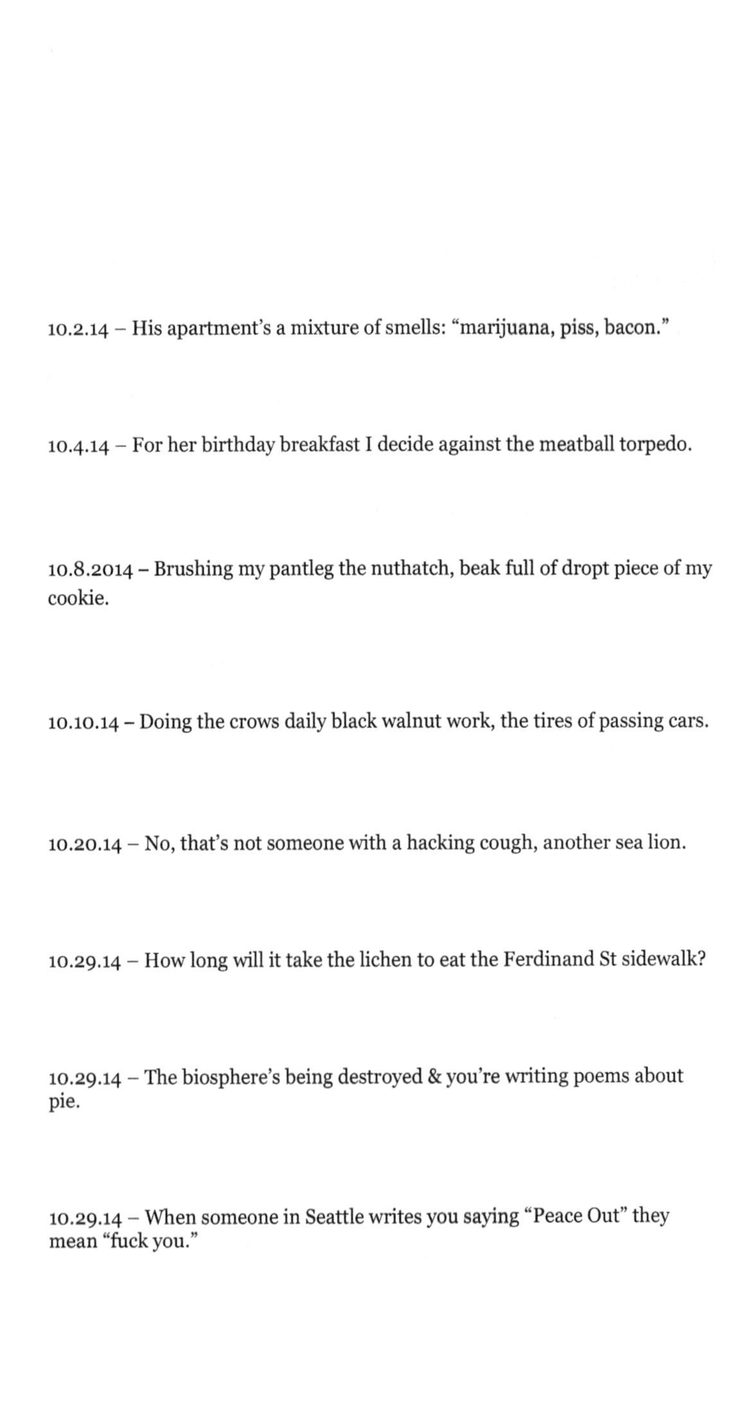

10.2.14 – His apartment's a mixture of smells: "marijuana, piss, bacon."

10.4.14 – For her birthday breakfast I decide against the meatball torpedo.

10.8.2014 – Brushing my pantleg the nuthatch, beak full of dropt piece of my cookie.

10.10.14 – Doing the crows daily black walnut work, the tires of passing cars.

10.20.14 – No, that's not someone with a hacking cough, another sea lion.

10.29.14 – How long will it take the lichen to eat the Ferdinand St sidewalk?

10.29.14 – The biosphere's being destroyed & you're writing poems about pie.

10.29.14 – When someone in Seattle writes you saying "Peace Out" they mean "fuck you."

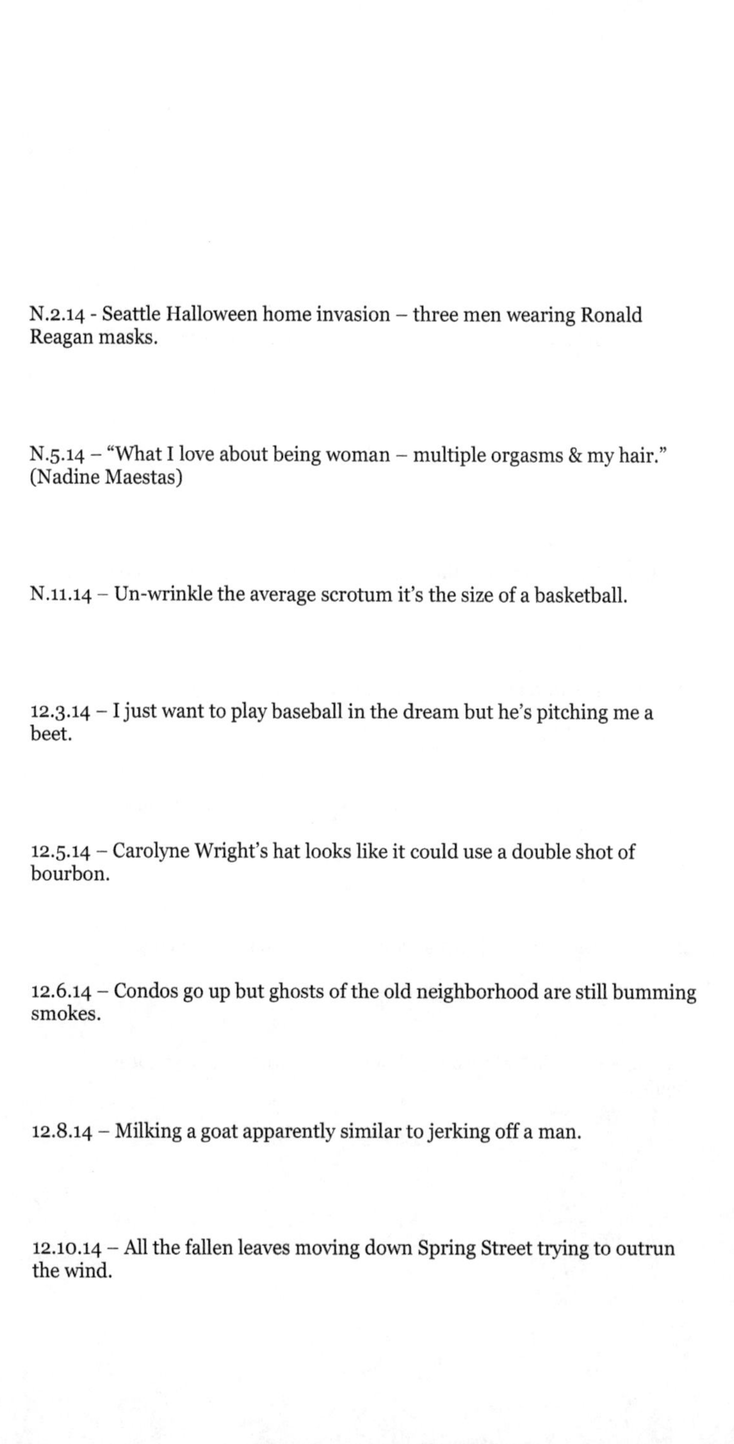

N.2.14 - Seattle Halloween home invasion – three men wearing Ronald Reagan masks.

N.5.14 – “What I love about being woman – multiple orgasms & my hair.” (Nadine Maestas)

N.11.14 – Un-wrinkle the average scrotum it’s the size of a basketball.

12.3.14 – I just want to play baseball in the dream but he’s pitching me a beet.

12.5.14 – Carolyne Wright’s hat looks like it could use a double shot of bourbon.

12.6.14 – Condos go up but ghosts of the old neighborhood are still bumming smokes.

12.8.14 – Milking a goat apparently similar to jerking off a man.

12.10.14 – All the fallen leaves moving down Spring Street trying to outrun the wind.

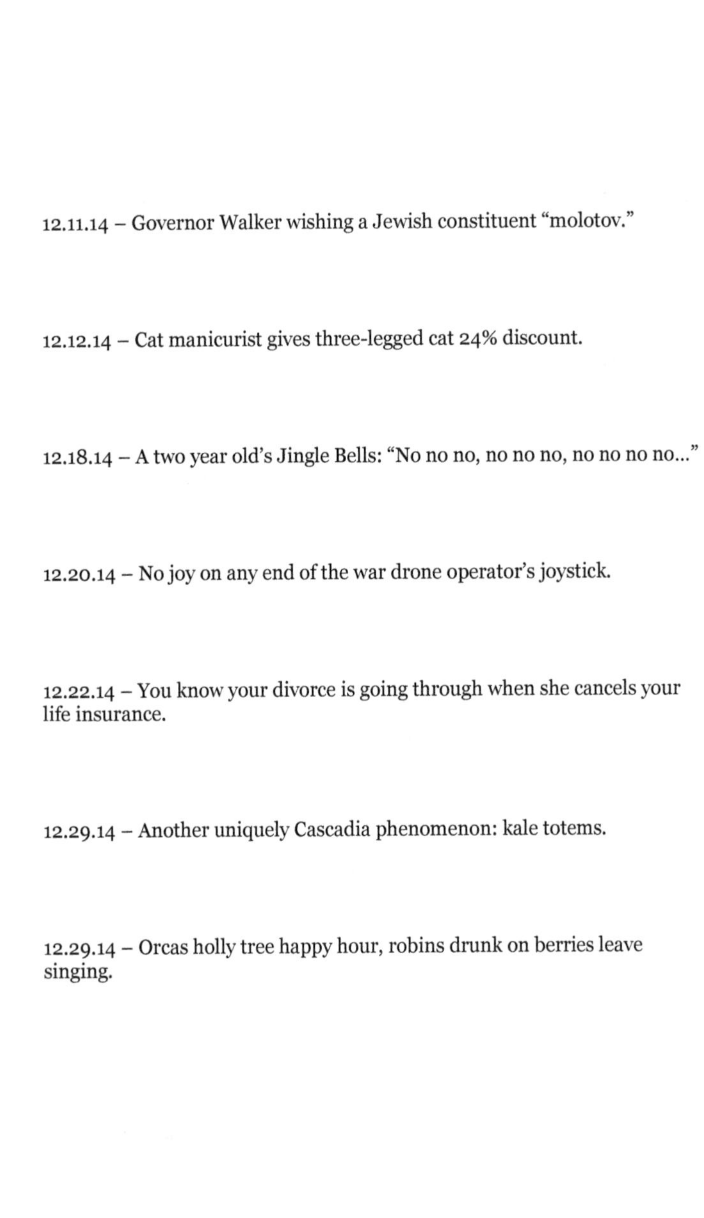

12.11.14 – Governor Walker wishing a Jewish constituent “molotov.”

12.12.14 – Cat manicurist gives three-legged cat 24% discount.

12.18.14 – A two year old’s Jingle Bells: “No no no, no no no, no no no no...”

12.20.14 – No joy on any end of the war drone operator’s joystick.

12.22.14 – You know your divorce is going through when she cancels your life insurance.

12.29.14 – Another uniquely Cascadia phenomenon: kale totems.

12.29.14 – Orcas holly tree happy hour, robins drunk on berries leave singing.

2015

1.2.15 – Perfect babysitters for a two & a half year old – Ren & Stimpy.

1.31.15 – Three-legged cat's attempted jabs fall short the length of one phantom limb.

2.4.15 – Joe on Whole Foods: "You have to take an escalator to buy an apple."

2.6.15 – How many worm obituaries end with the word "Sidewalk?"

2.21.15 – Carla Bley gets ideas for melodies listening to chickens.

3.6.15 – Who are the three idiot who voted thumb's down on Coltrane's Olé?

3.9.15 – After the dentist Ted says: "walk out w/ a house payment in my mouth!"

3.11.15 – This guy needs a new transmission & I'm not talking about his car!

3.21.15 – Sprouts, french fries and worm ranches – a history of Subud enterprises.

3.23.15 – On the Facebook thread about critical discourse, he puts frowny face.

3.26.15 – They drain Lake Tapps to find beer cans, tires & Sammy Hagar cassette.

3.26.2015 – "A poem, mine or another's, is an occult document." (Duncan)

3.27.2015 – An anagram for Brenda Hillman is, sorry Bob, "In Man Bard Hell."

3.28.2015 – The cats can cry all they want but they won't be fed 'til we're done fucking.

4.2.2015 – "Kale's not food" says Sam whose breakfast was pastry, coffee and a smoke.

4.3.2015 – Sam tells me: "Reading Zukovsky is like doing a crossword puzzle."

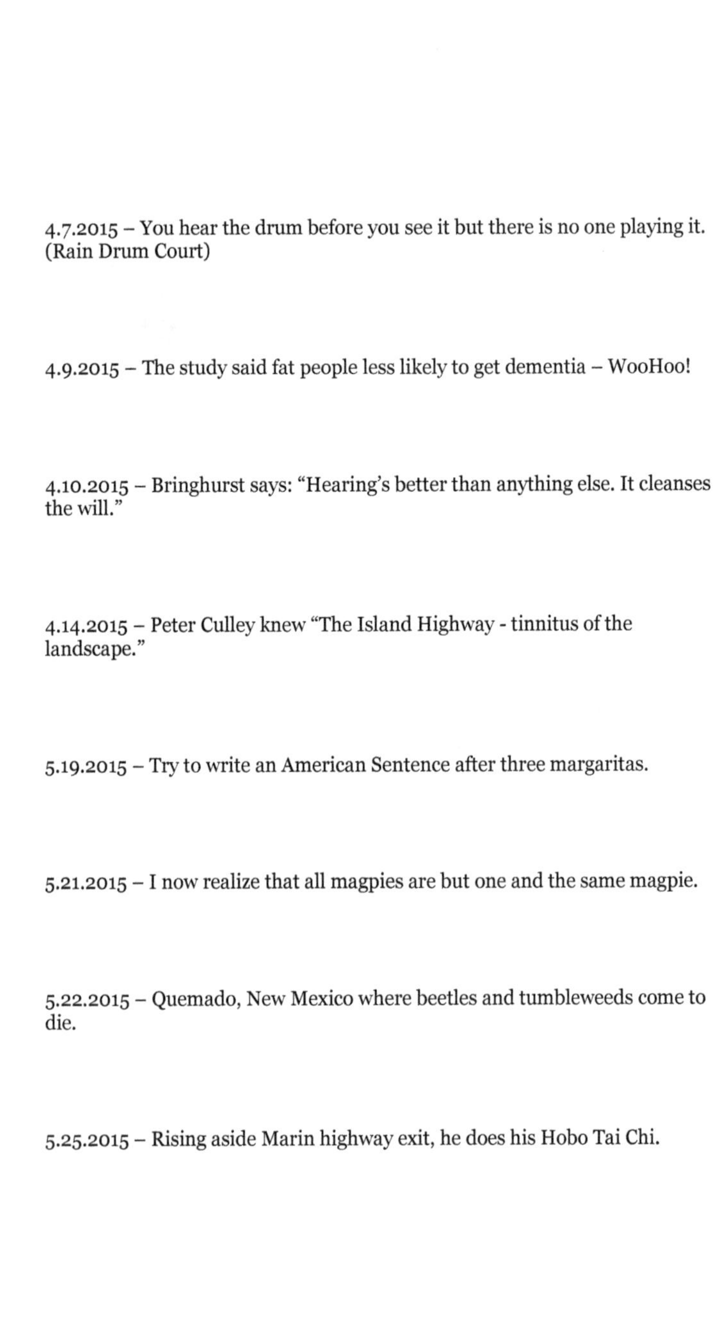

4.7.2015 – You hear the drum before you see it but there is no one playing it. (Rain Drum Court)

4.9.2015 – The study said fat people less likely to get dementia – WooHoo!

4.10.2015 – Bringhurst says: “Hearing’s better than anything else. It cleanses the will.”

4.14.2015 – Peter Culley knew “The Island Highway - tinnitus of the landscape.”

5.19.2015 – Try to write an American Sentence after three margaritas.

5.21.2015 – I now realize that all magpies are but one and the same magpie.

5.22.2015 – Quemado, New Mexico where beetles and tumbleweeds come to die.

5.25.2015 – Rising aside Marin highway exit, he does his Hobo Tai Chi.

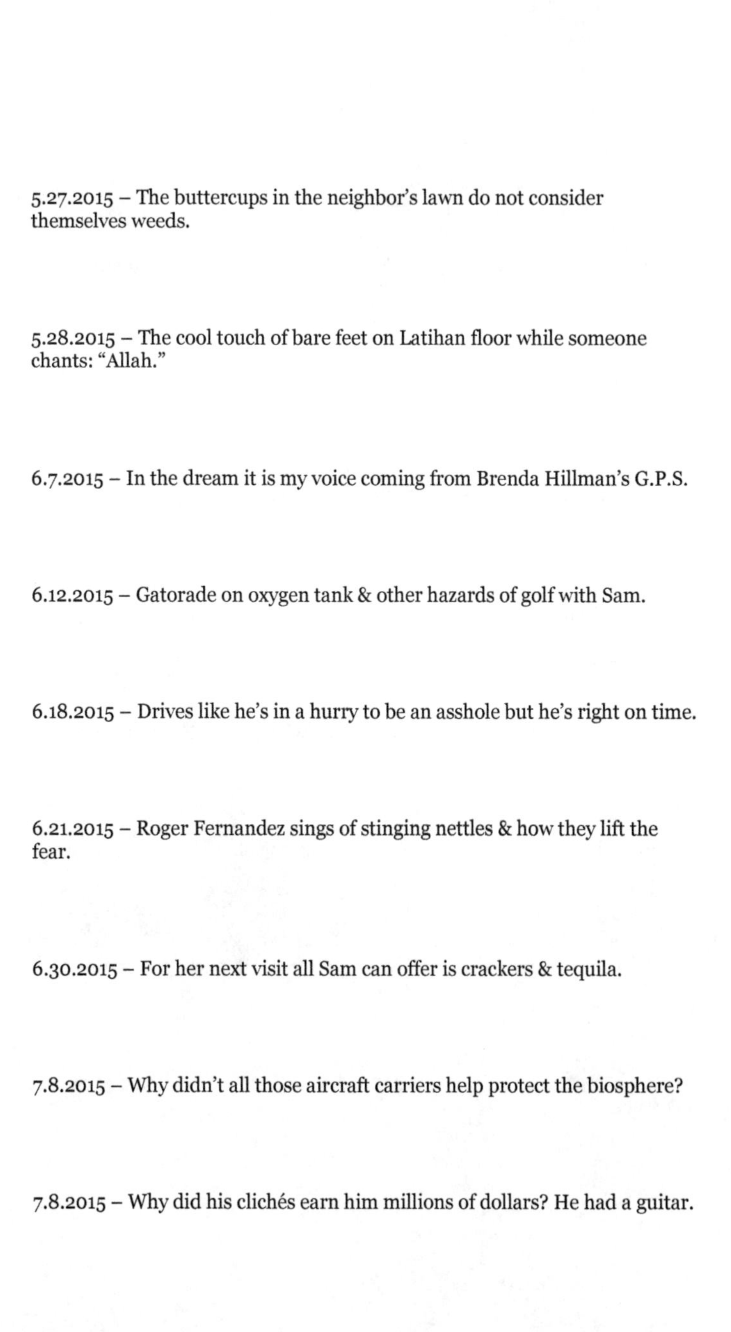

5.27.2015 – The buttercups in the neighbor's lawn do not consider themselves weeds.

5.28.2015 – The cool touch of bare feet on Latihan floor while someone chants: "Allah."

6.7.2015 – In the dream it is my voice coming from Brenda Hillman's G.P.S.

6.12.2015 – Gatorade on oxygen tank & other hazards of golf with Sam.

6.18.2015 – Drives like he's in a hurry to be an asshole but he's right on time.

6.21.2015 – Roger Fernandez sings of stinging nettles & how they lift the fear.

6.30.2015 – For her next visit all Sam can offer is crackers & tequila.

7.8.2015 – Why didn't all those aircraft carriers help protect the biosphere?

7.8.2015 – Why did his clichés earn him millions of dollars? He had a guitar.

7.12.2015 – We are relieved when it's a campfire ban and not a caffeine ban.

7.31.15 – One of those days where I read the blender's brand as "Ostracizer."

8.10.15 – Neglected, the city would be a forest of chicory & horsetail.

8.13.15 – All of the German words I know I learned from Hogan's Heroes.

9.7.15 – On 101 she spots Red Hot Pokers growing next to Naked Ladies.

9.15.15 – Bhakti searches for broken hobos playing oboes in Hoboken.

9.23.15 – Entitlement parks her large American car in 3 reserved spots.

9.30.15 – The falling ash leaf – as if it had second thoughts – clings to chain link fence.

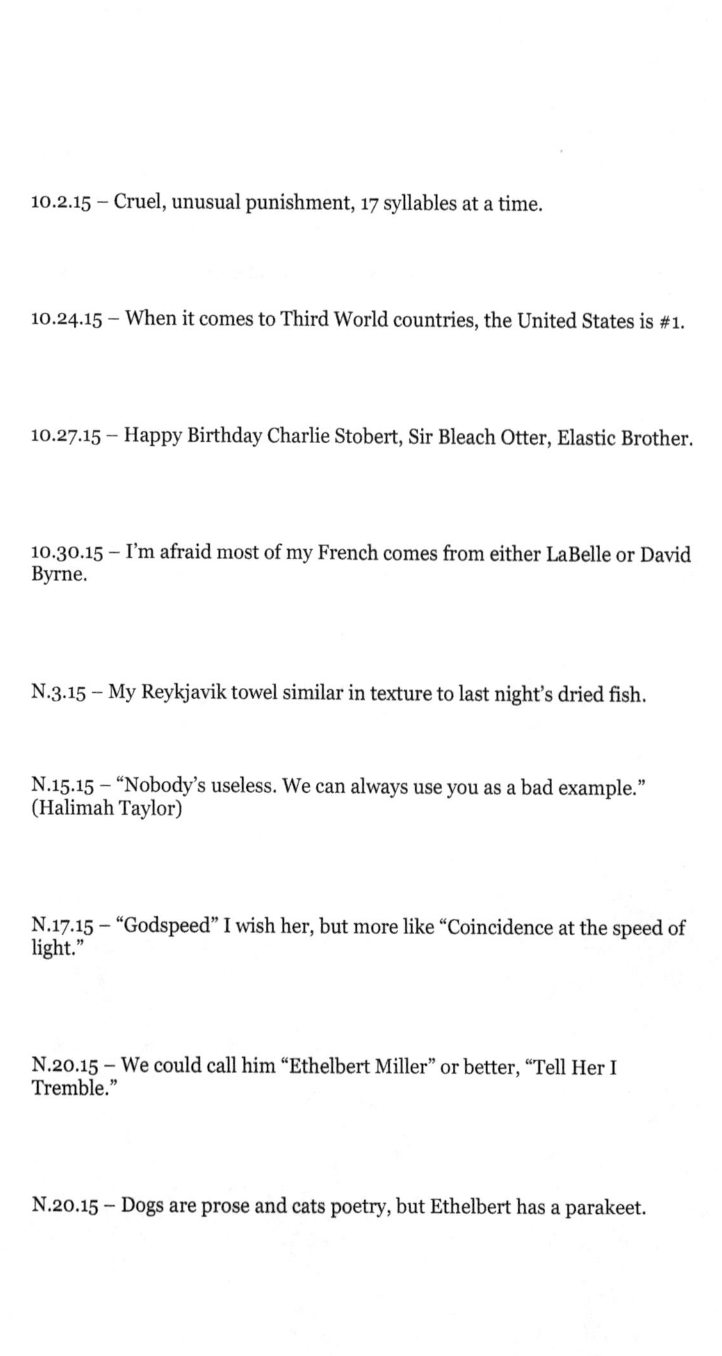

10.2.15 – Cruel, unusual punishment, 17 syllables at a time.

10.24.15 – When it comes to Third World countries, the United States is #1.

10.27.15 – Happy Birthday Charlie Stobert, Sir Bleach Otter, Elastic Brother.

10.30.15 – I'm afraid most of my French comes from either LaBelle or David Byrne.

N.3.15 – My Reykjavik towel similar in texture to last night's dried fish.

N.15.15 – "Nobody's useless. We can always use you as a bad example." (Halimah Taylor)

N.17.15 – "Godspeed" I wish her, but more like "Coincidence at the speed of light."

N.20.15 – We could call him "Ethelbert Miller" or better, "Tell Her I Tremble."

N.20.15 – Dogs are prose and cats poetry, but Ethelbert has a parakeet.

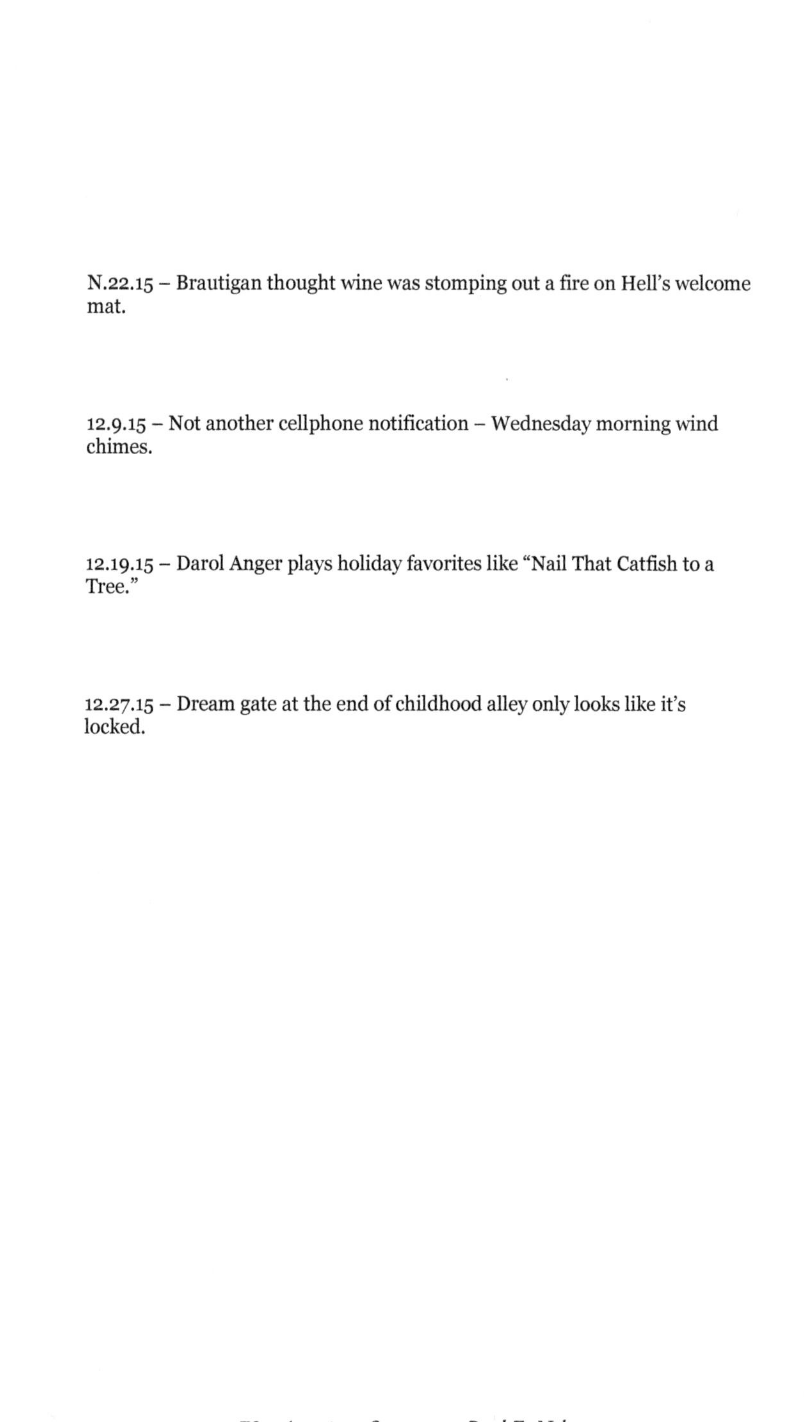

N.22.15 – Brautigan thought wine was stomping out a fire on Hell's welcome mat.

12.9.15 – Not another cellphone notification – Wednesday morning wind chimes.

12.19.15 – Darol Anger plays holiday favorites like "Nail That Catfish to a Tree."

12.27.15 – Dream gate at the end of childhood alley only looks like it's locked.

2016

1.13.16 – After Canadian Punjabi meal we feel like $800 thousand bucks.

1.16.16 – Saundra Fleming is a Farmland Genius who has Flaming Adrenals.

1.19.16 – Until Ella gets clarity with her fricatives it's "Posty the Towman."

1.26.16 – Today's sign in Flint, Michigan: "Family Fun Night & Lead Testing."

2.14.16 – What's the message when a hummingbird drops out of the sky as you walk?

2.26.16 – Closed Caption at Republican debate: "Unintelligible Yelling."

3.2.16 – Fortunately I never told the French I was going to be a star.

3.9.16 – If you did come back as a hummingbird don't fly so close to my face.

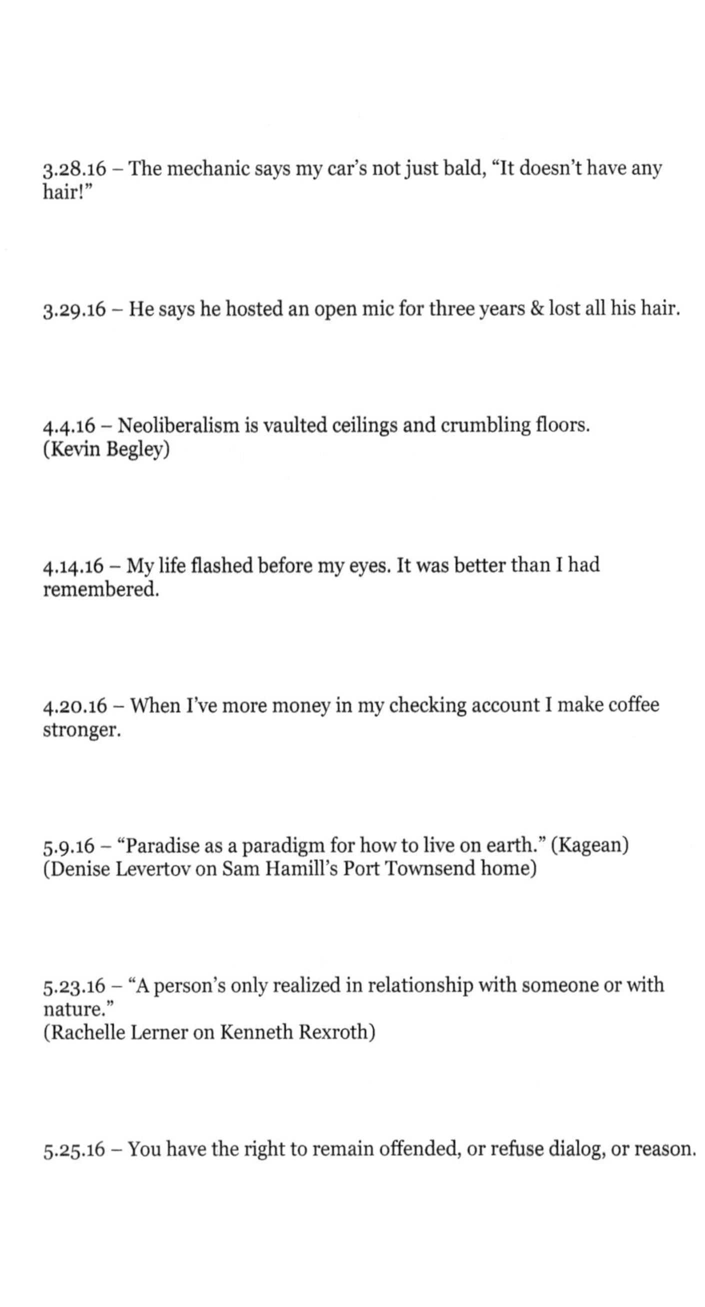

3.28.16 – The mechanic says my car's not just bald, "It doesn't have any hair!"

3.29.16 – He says he hosted an open mic for three years & lost all his hair.

4.4.16 – Neoliberalism is vaulted ceilings and crumbling floors.
(Kevin Begley)

4.14.16 – My life flashed before my eyes. It was better than I had remembered.

4.20.16 – When I've more money in my checking account I make coffee stronger.

5.9.16 – "Paradise as a paradigm for how to live on earth." (Kagean)
(Denise Levertov on Sam Hamill's Port Townsend home)

5.23.16 – "A person's only realized in relationship with someone or with nature."
(Rachelle Lerner on Kenneth Rexroth)

5.25.16 – You have the right to remain offended, or refuse dialog, or reason.

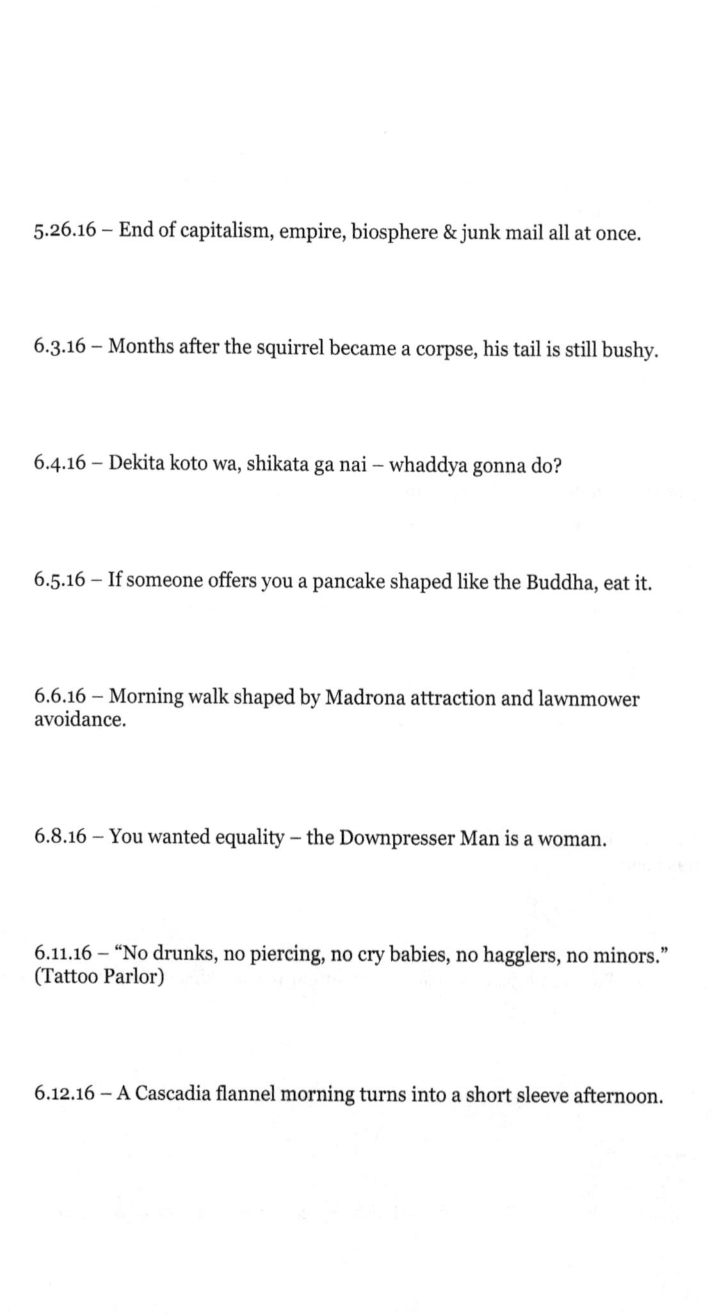

5.26.16 – End of capitalism, empire, biosphere & junk mail all at once.

6.3.16 – Months after the squirrel became a corpse, his tail is still bushy.

6.4.16 – Dekita koto wa, shikata ga nai – whaddya gonna do?

6.5.16 – If someone offers you a pancake shaped like the Buddha, eat it.

6.6.16 – Morning walk shaped by Madrona attraction and lawnmower avoidance.

6.8.16 – You wanted equality – the Downpresser Man is a woman.

6.11.16 – “No drunks, no piercing, no cry babies, no hagglers, no minors.” (Tattoo Parlor)

6.12.16 – A Cascadia flannel morning turns into a short sleeve afternoon.

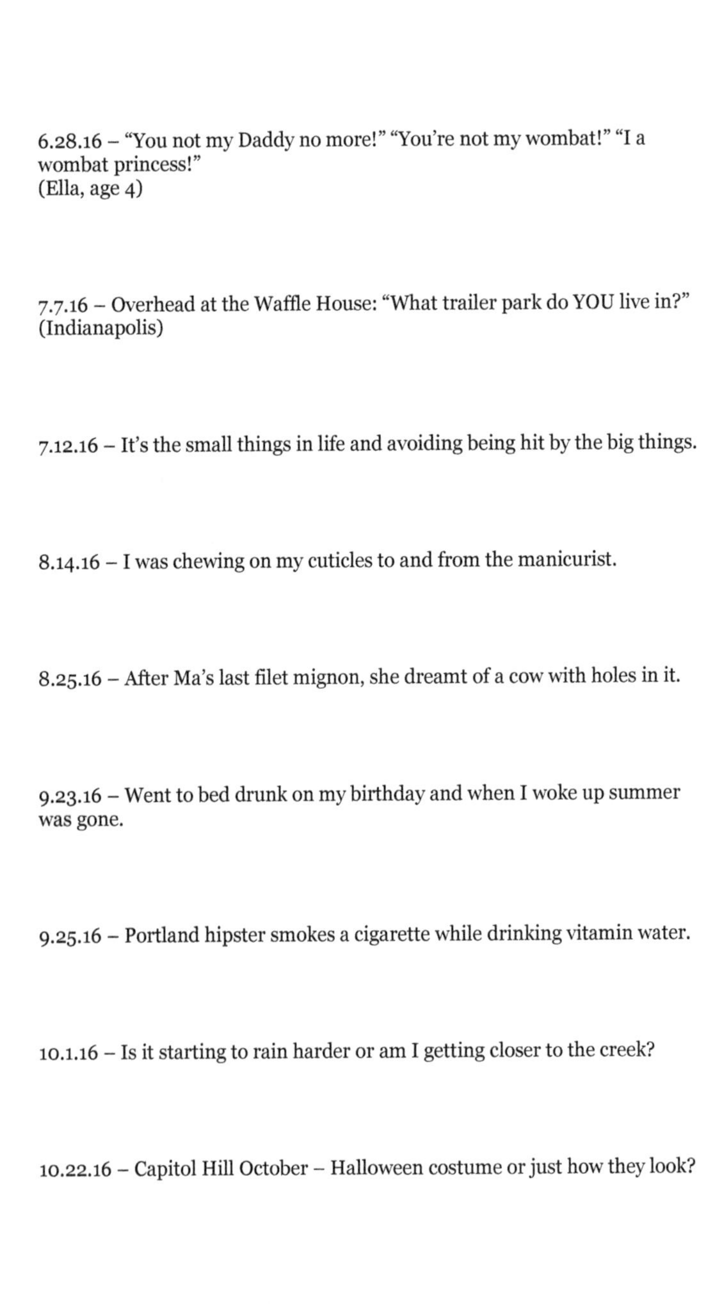

6.28.16 – “You not my Daddy no more!” “You’re not my wombat!” “I a wombat princess!”
(Ella, age 4)

7.7.16 – Overhead at the Waffle House: “What trailer park do YOU live in?”
(Indianapolis)

7.12.16 – It’s the small things in life and avoiding being hit by the big things.

8.14.16 – I was chewing on my cuticles to and from the manicurist.

8.25.16 – After Ma’s last filet mignon, she dreamt of a cow with holes in it.

9.23.16 – Went to bed drunk on my birthday and when I woke up summer was gone.

9.25.16 – Portland hipster smokes a cigarette while drinking vitamin water.

10.1.16 – Is it starting to rain harder or am I getting closer to the creek?

10.22.16 – Capitol Hill October – Halloween costume or just how they look?

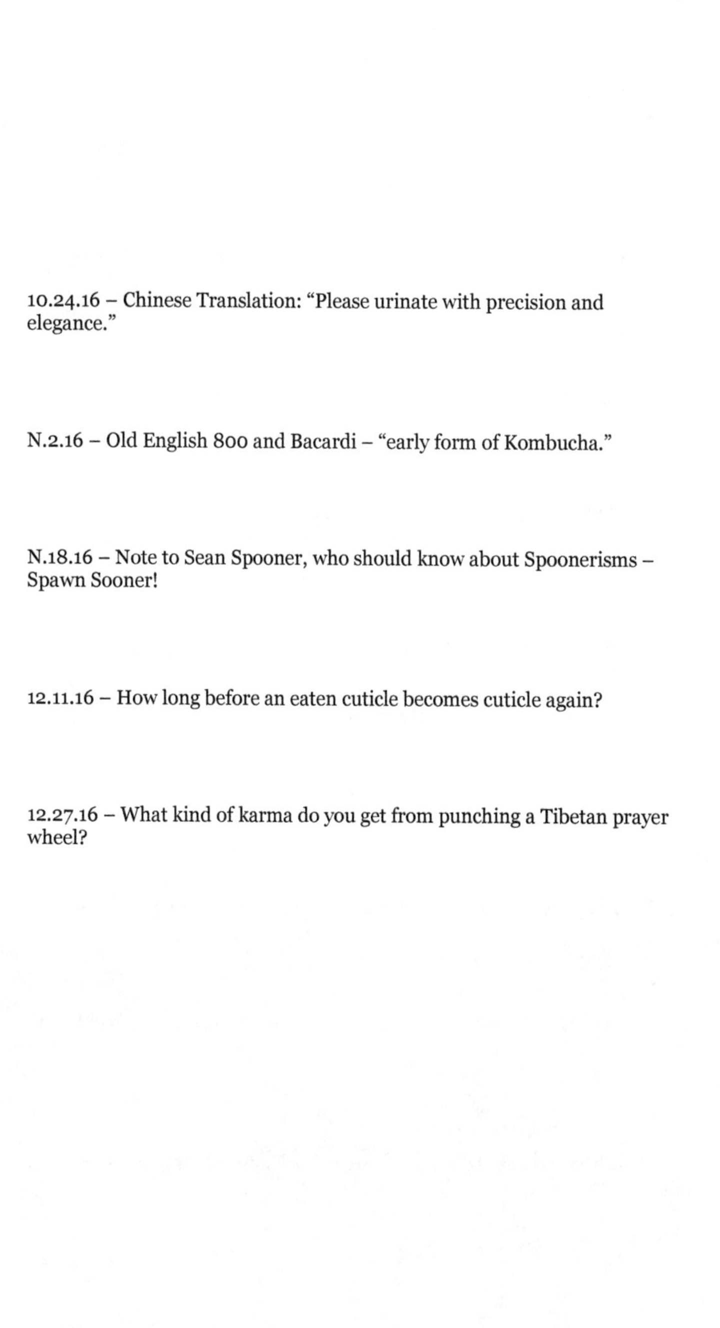

10.24.16 – Chinese Translation: “Please urinate with precision and elegance.”

N.2.16 – Old English 800 and Bacardi – “early form of Kombucha.”

N.18.16 – Note to Sean Spooner, who should know about Spoonerisms – Spawn Sooner!

12.11.16 – How long before an eaten cuticle becomes cuticle again?

12.27.16 – What kind of karma do you get from punching a Tibetan prayer wheel?

2017

1.7.17 – Newsthump says Donald Trump to be sworn in on book of carpet samples.

2.8.17 – Spiders can't get outta sinks, palmetto bugs can't get outta bathtubs.

2.11.17 – Everything that goes into my vest pocket comes out stained – even ghosts.

2.22.17 – Why won't the leaf-turning crow just go to the sidewalk for stranded worms?

3.4.17 – José won't call him "45" – El Caudillo Analfabético.

3.4.17 – Takes a Canadian woman to get golf elbow from chopping wood.

3.12.17 – To call out small portions Pop would say: "That's not enough to put in your eye!"

4.14.17 – Ilya writes at night how he "steals back into the margins of his skin."

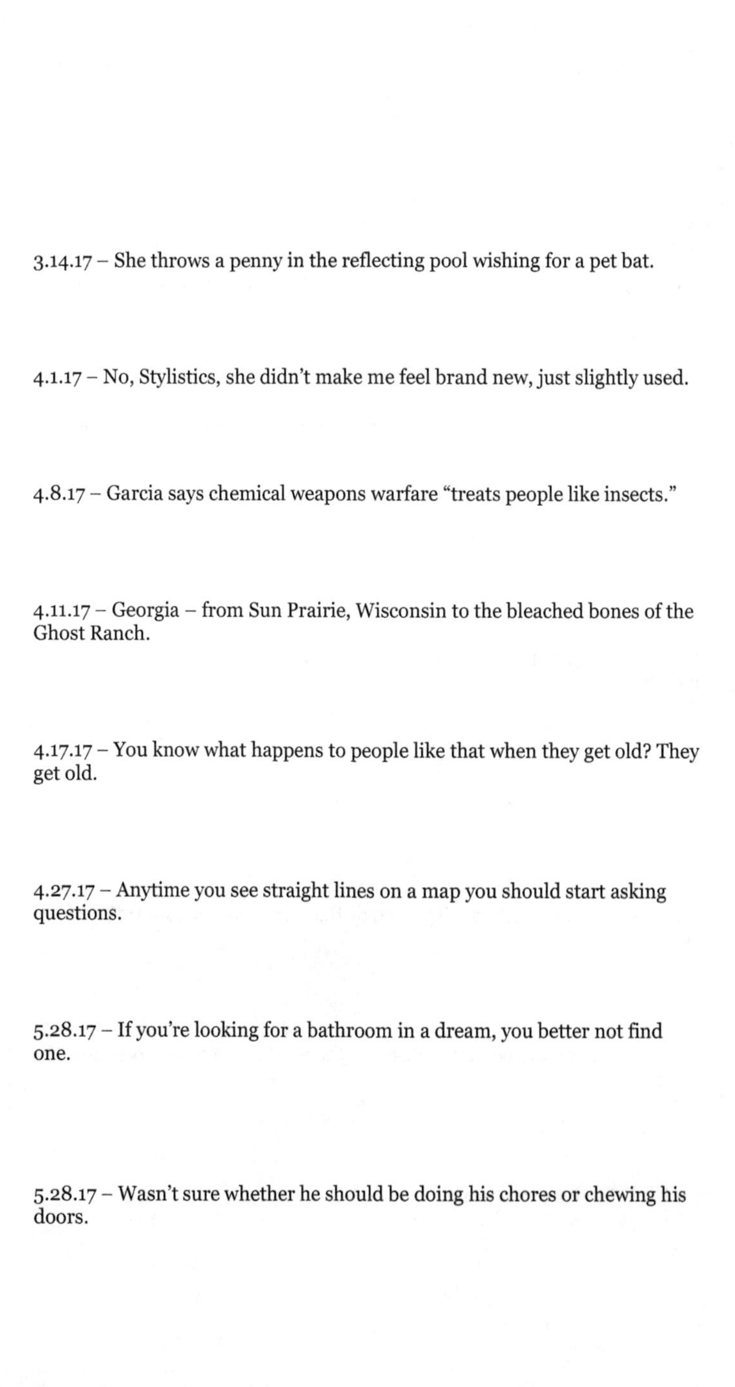

3.14.17 – She throws a penny in the reflecting pool wishing for a pet bat.

4.1.17 – No, Stylistics, she didn't make me feel brand new, just slightly used.

4.8.17 – Garcia says chemical weapons warfare "treats people like insects."

4.11.17 – Georgia – from Sun Prairie, Wisconsin to the bleached bones of the Ghost Ranch.

4.17.17 – You know what happens to people like that when they get old? They get old.

4.27.17 – Anytime you see straight lines on a map you should start asking questions.

5.28.17 – If you're looking for a bathroom in a dream, you better not find one.

5.28.17 – Wasn't sure whether he should be doing his chores or chewing his doors.

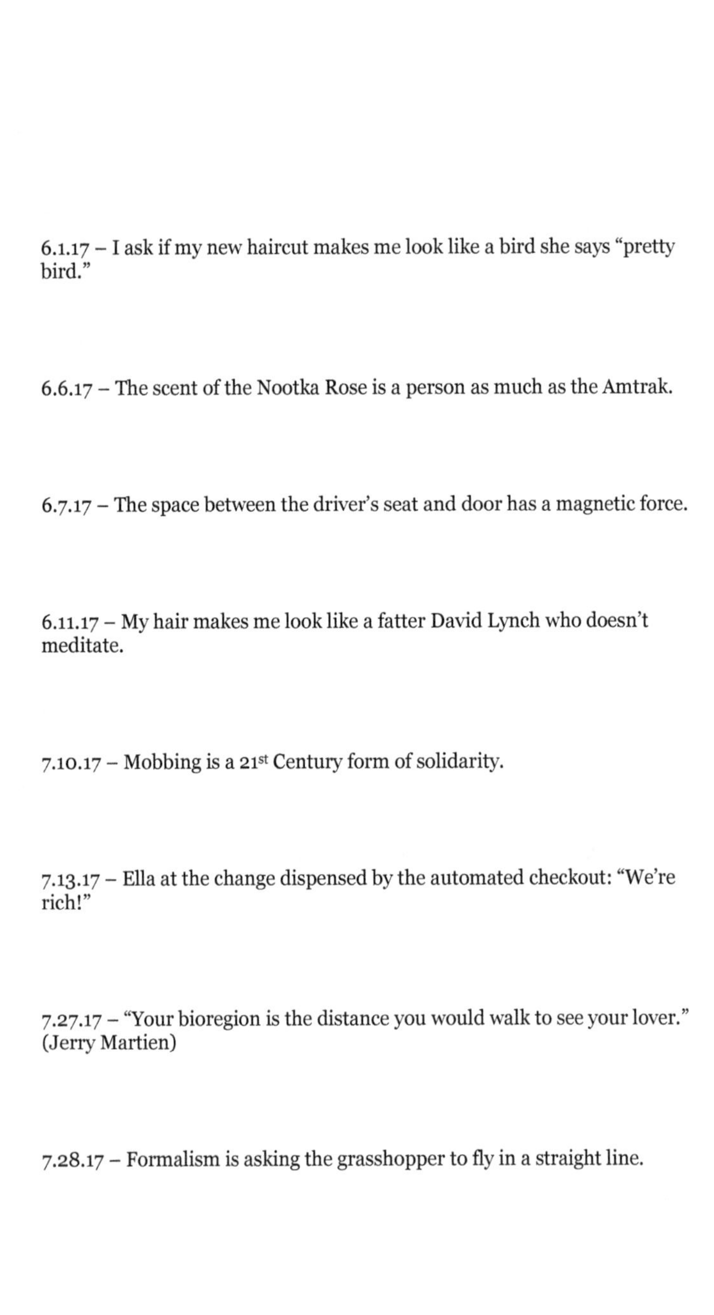

6.1.17 – I ask if my new haircut makes me look like a bird she says "pretty bird."

6.6.17 – The scent of the Nootka Rose is a person as much as the Amtrak.

6.7.17 – The space between the driver's seat and door has a magnetic force.

6.11.17 – My hair makes me look like a fatter David Lynch who doesn't meditate.

7.10.17 – Mobbing is a 21st Century form of solidarity.

7.13.17 – Ella at the change dispensed by the automated checkout: "We're rich!"

7.27.17 – "Your bioregion is the distance you would walk to see your lover." (Jerry Martien)

7.28.17 – Formalism is asking the grasshopper to fly in a straight line.

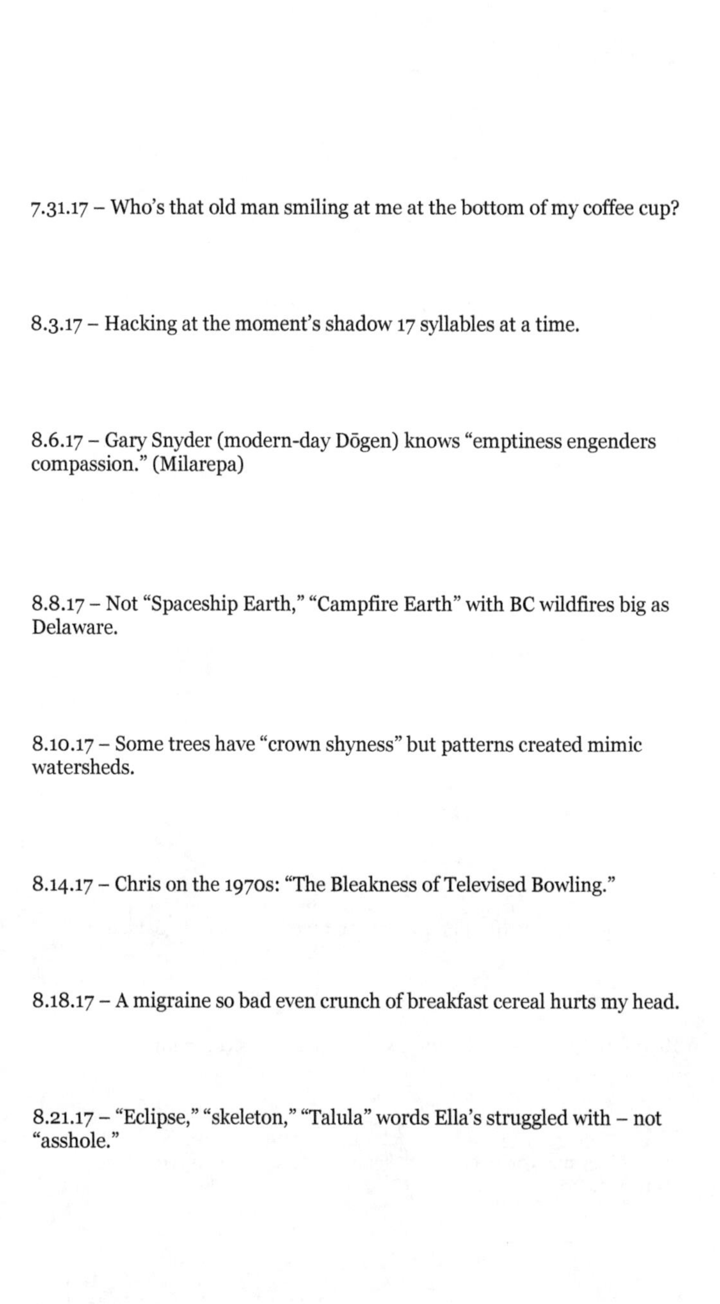

7.31.17 – Who's that old man smiling at me at the bottom of my coffee cup?

8.3.17 – Hacking at the moment's shadow 17 syllables at a time.

8.6.17 – Gary Snyder (modern-day Dōgen) knows "emptiness engenders compassion." (Milarepa)

8.8.17 – Not "Spaceship Earth," "Campfire Earth" with BC wildfires big as Delaware.

8.10.17 – Some trees have "crown shyness" but patterns created mimic watersheds.

8.14.17 – Chris on the 1970s: "The Bleakness of Televised Bowling."

8.18.17 – A migraine so bad even crunch of breakfast cereal hurts my head.

8.21.17 – "Eclipse," "skeleton," "Talula" words Ella's struggled with – not "asshole."

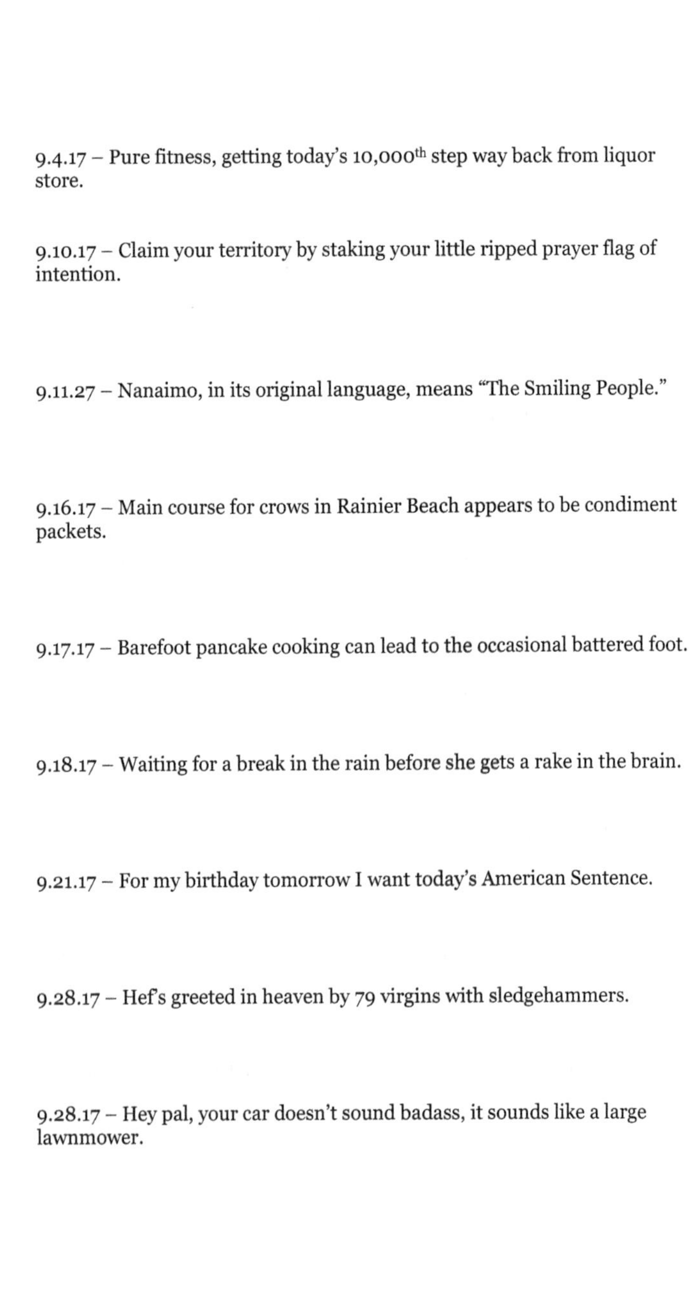

9.4.17 – Pure fitness, getting today's 10,000th step way back from liquor store.

9.10.17 – Claim your territory by staking your little ripped prayer flag of intention.

9.11.27 – Nanaimo, in its original language, means "The Smiling People."

9.16.17 – Main course for crows in Rainier Beach appears to be condiment packets.

9.17.17 – Barefoot pancake cooking can lead to the occasional battered foot.

9.18.17 – Waiting for a break in the rain before she gets a rake in the brain.

9.21.17 – For my birthday tomorrow I want today's American Sentence.

9.28.17 – Hef's greeted in heaven by 79 virgins with sledgehammers.

9.28.17 – Hey pal, your car doesn't sound badass, it sounds like a large lawnmower.

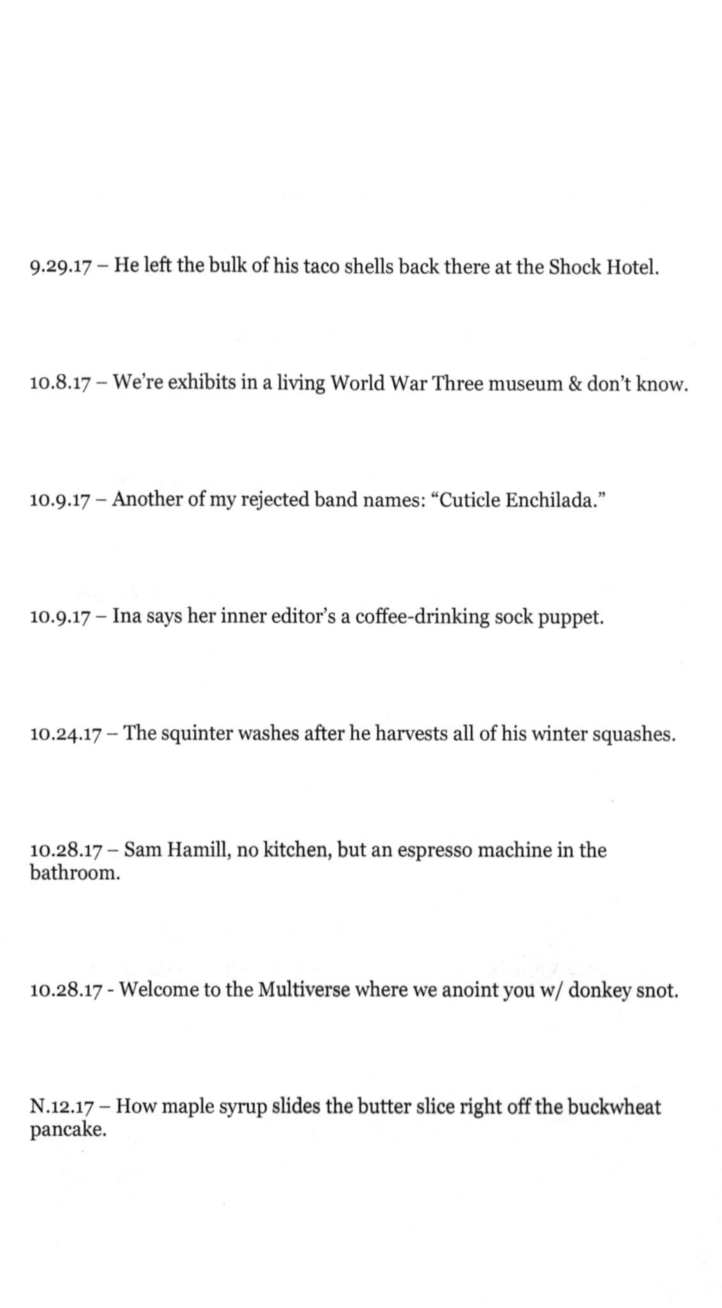

9.29.17 – He left the bulk of his taco shells back there at the Shock Hotel.

10.8.17 – We're exhibits in a living World War Three museum & don't know.

10.9.17 – Another of my rejected band names: "Cuticle Enchilada."

10.9.17 – Ina says her inner editor's a coffee-drinking sock puppet.

10.24.17 – The squinter washes after he harvests all of his winter squashes.

10.28.17 – Sam Hamill, no kitchen, but an espresso machine in the bathroom.

10.28.17 - Welcome to the Multiverse where we anoint you w/ donkey snot.

N.12.17 – How maple syrup slides the butter slice right off the buckwheat pancake.

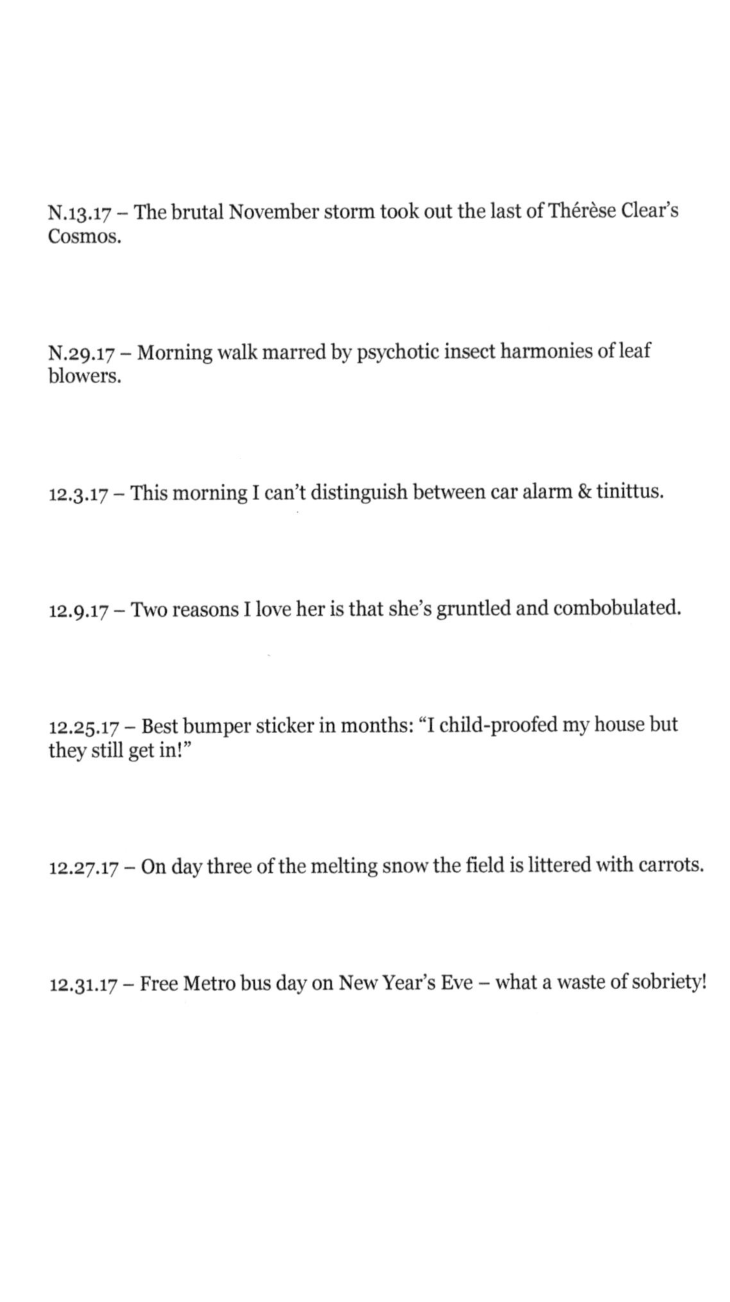

N.13.17 – The brutal November storm took out the last of Thérèse Clear's Cosmos.

N.29.17 – Morning walk marred by psychotic insect harmonies of leaf blowers.

12.3.17 – This morning I can't distinguish between car alarm & tinittus.

12.9.17 – Two reasons I love her is that she's gruntled and combobulated.

12.25.17 – Best bumper sticker in months: "I child-proofed my house but they still get in!"

12.27.17 – On day three of the melting snow the field is littered with carrots.

12.31.17 – Free Metro bus day on New Year's Eve – what a waste of sobriety!

2018

1.11.18 – Walking meditation, focus on getting credit for all my steps.

1.16.18 – Ella says she wants to visit Egypt and make a pet mummy friend.

1.23.18 – Restaurant with Chinese-Canadian cuisine has duck neck poutine.

1.27.18 – Only spellcheck would think I'd want to wish someone a "hasty mañana."

2.1.17 – Ikea's founder died – took three hours to assemble his coffin.

2.16.18 – My proposed tombstone epitaph: "So THIS is how you stop tinittus!"

2.21.18 – Andrew Schelling says he's a "lapsed Buddhist with multiple belongings."

2.23.18 – Joanne could make elegant serving snacks she got on an airplane flight. (Andrew Schelling on Joanne Kyger)

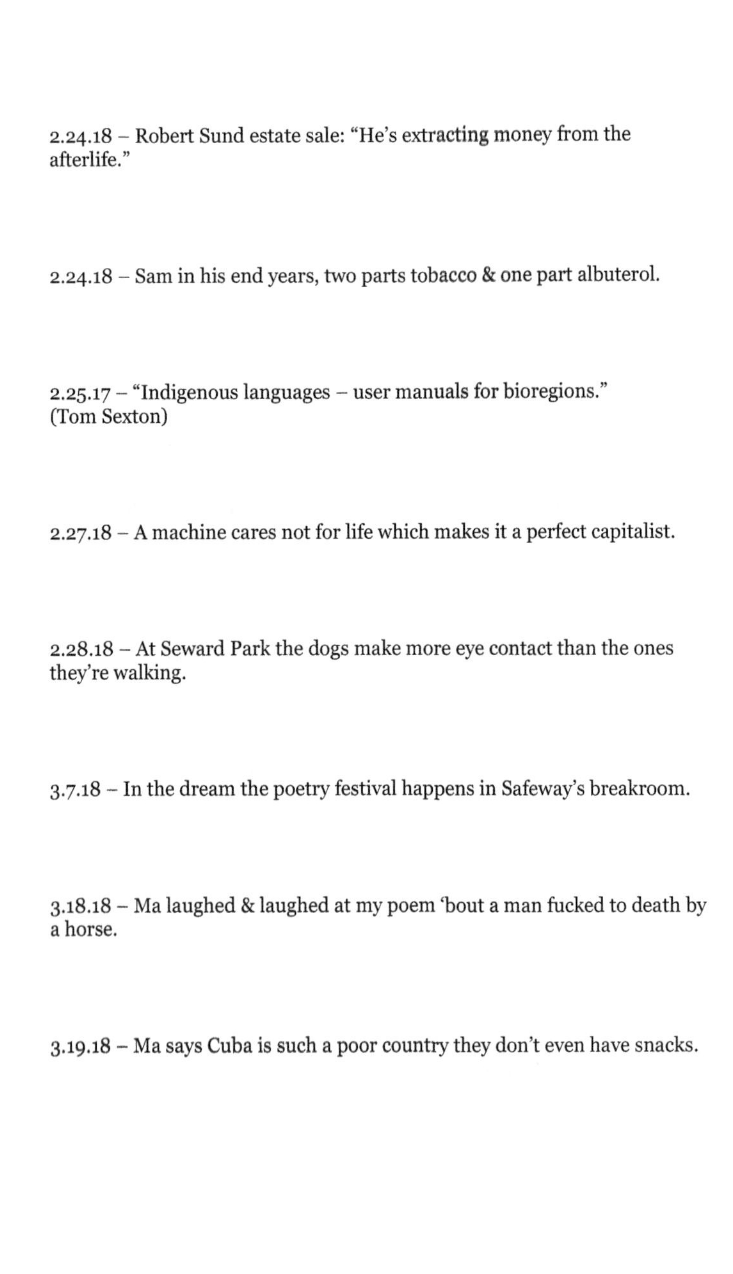

2.24.18 – Robert Sund estate sale: "He's extracting money from the afterlife."

2.24.18 – Sam in his end years, two parts tobacco & one part albuterol.

2.25.17 – "Indigenous languages – user manuals for bioregions." (Tom Sexton)

2.27.18 – A machine cares not for life which makes it a perfect capitalist.

2.28.18 – At Seward Park the dogs make more eye contact than the ones they're walking.

3.7.18 – In the dream the poetry festival happens in Safeway's breakroom.

3.18.18 – Ma laughed & laughed at my poem 'bout a man fucked to death by a horse.

3.19.18 – Ma says Cuba is such a poor country they don't even have snacks.

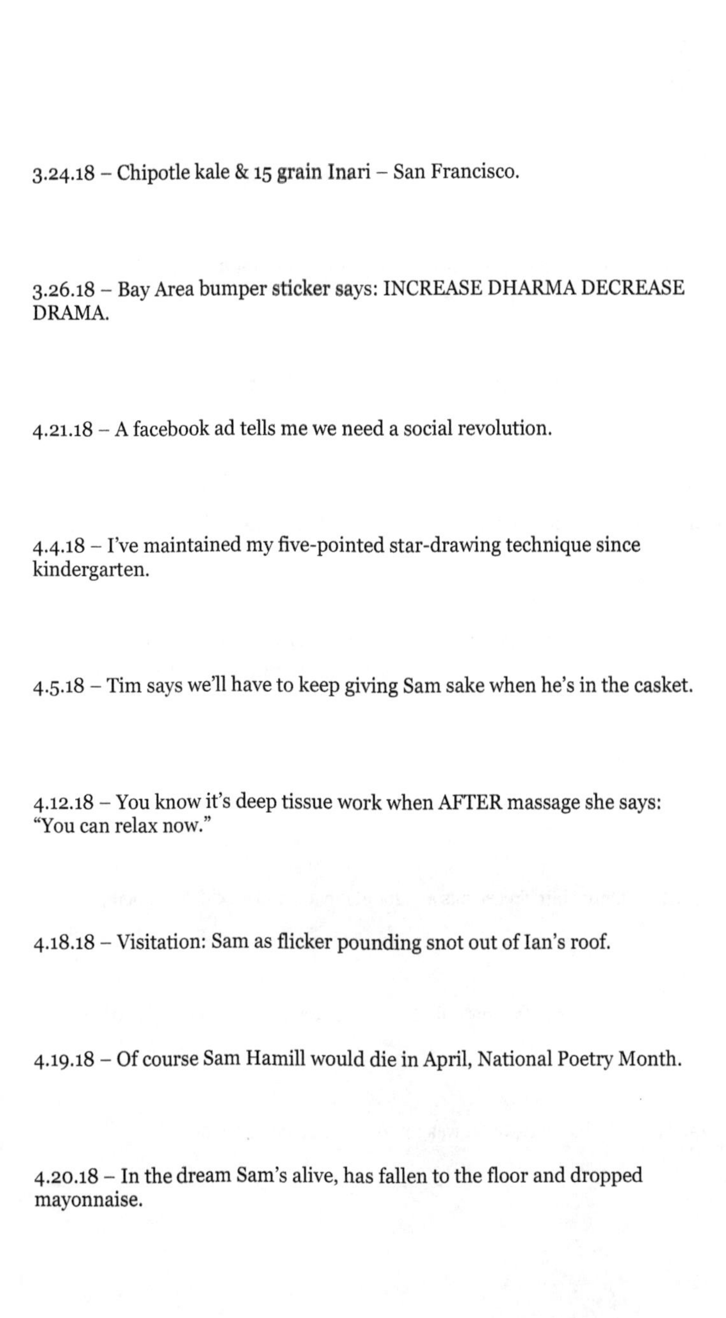

3.24.18 – Chipotle kale & 15 grain Inari – San Francisco.

3.26.18 – Bay Area bumper sticker says: INCREASE DHARMA DECREASE DRAMA.

4.21.18 – A facebook ad tells me we need a social revolution.

4.4.18 – I've maintained my five-pointed star-drawing technique since kindergarten.

4.5.18 – Tim says we'll have to keep giving Sam sake when he's in the casket.

4.12.18 – You know it's deep tissue work when AFTER massage she says: "You can relax now."

4.18.18 – Visitation: Sam as flicker pounding snot out of Ian's roof.

4.19.18 – Of course Sam Hamill would die in April, National Poetry Month.

4.20.18 – In the dream Sam's alive, has fallen to the floor and dropped mayonnaise.

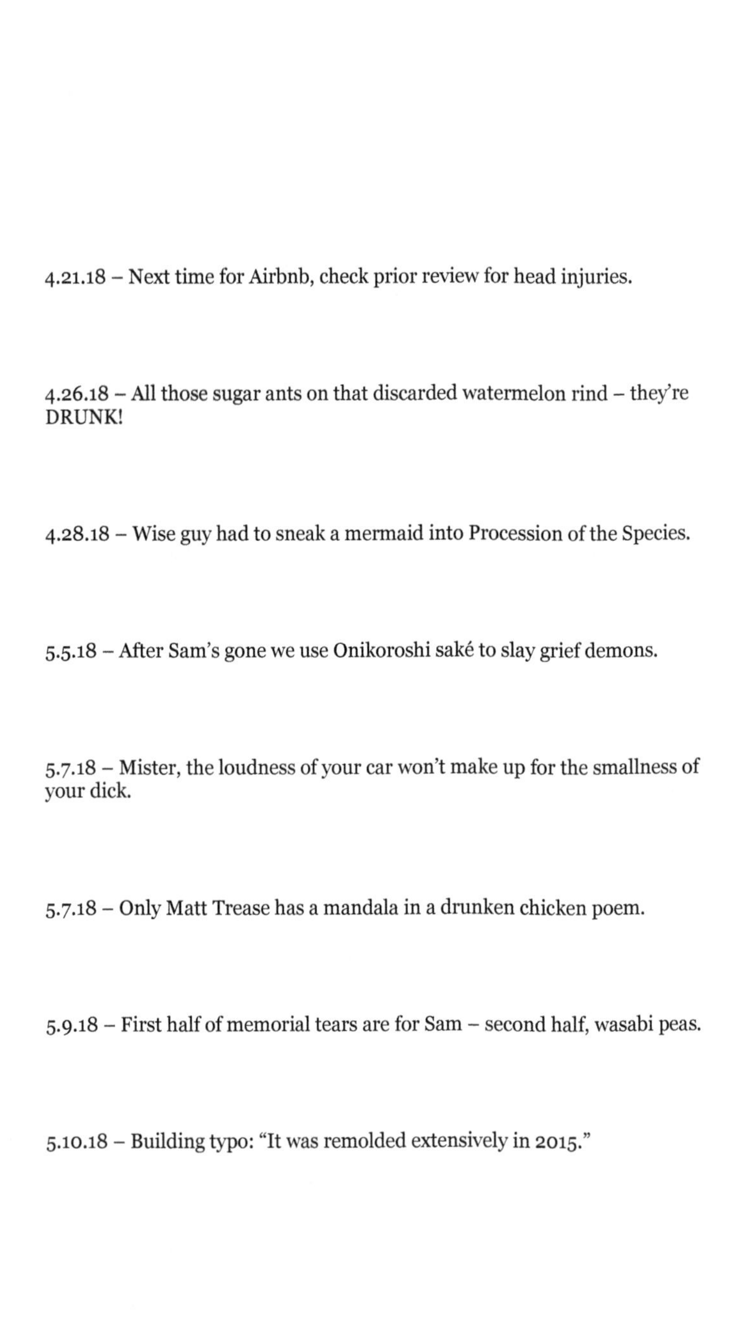

4.21.18 – Next time for Airbnb, check prior review for head injuries.

4.26.18 – All those sugar ants on that discarded watermelon rind – they're DRUNK!

4.28.18 – Wise guy had to sneak a mermaid into Procession of the Species.

5.5.18 – After Sam's gone we use Onikoroshi saké to slay grief demons.

5.7.18 – Mister, the loudness of your car won't make up for the smallness of your dick.

5.7.18 – Only Matt Trease has a mandala in a drunken chicken poem.

5.9.18 – First half of memorial tears are for Sam – second half, wasabi peas.

5.10.18 – Building typo: "It was remolded extensively in 2015."

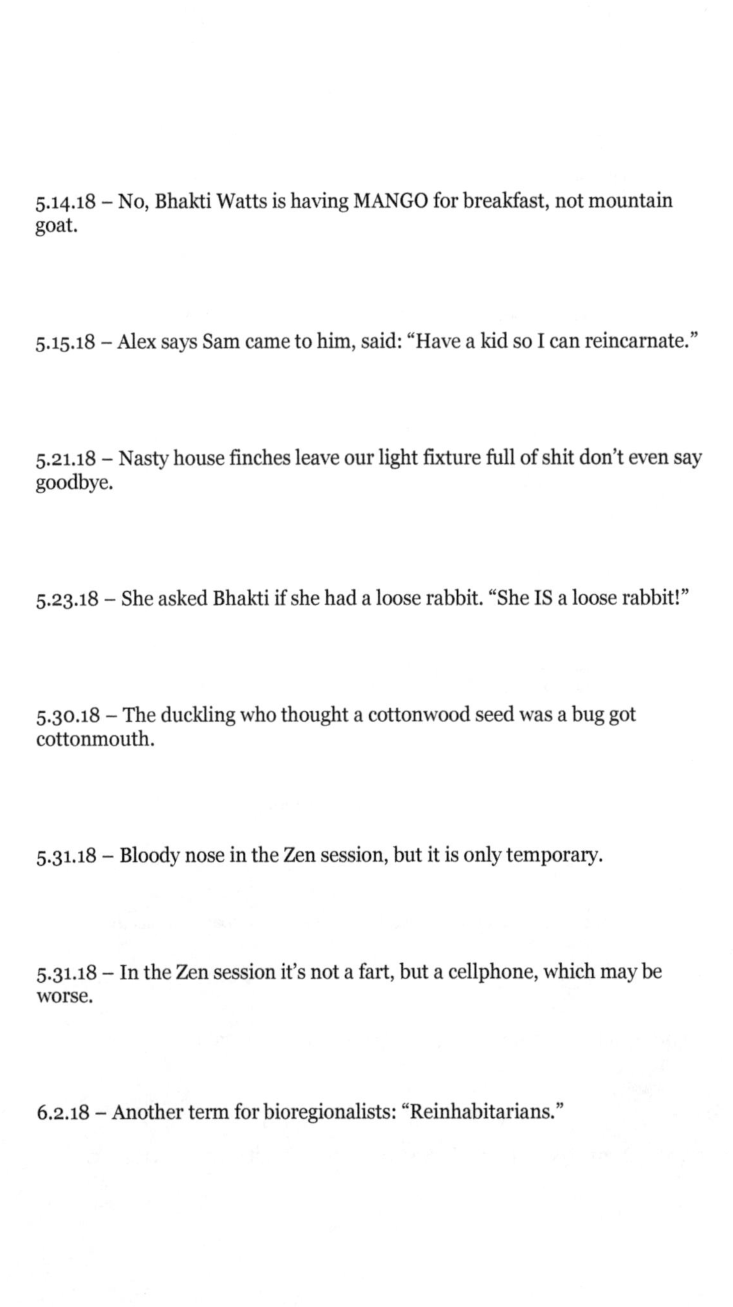

5.14.18 – No, Bhakti Watts is having MANGO for breakfast, not mountain goat.

5.15.18 – Alex says Sam came to him, said: “Have a kid so I can reincarnate.”

5.21.18 – Nasty house finches leave our light fixture full of shit don’t even say goodbye.

5.23.18 – She asked Bhakti if she had a loose rabbit. “She IS a loose rabbit!”

5.30.18 – The duckling who thought a cottonwood seed was a bug got cottonmouth.

5.31.18 – Bloody nose in the Zen session, but it is only temporary.

5.31.18 – In the Zen session it’s not a fart, but a cellphone, which may be worse.

6.2.18 – Another term for bioregionalists: “Reinhabitarians.”

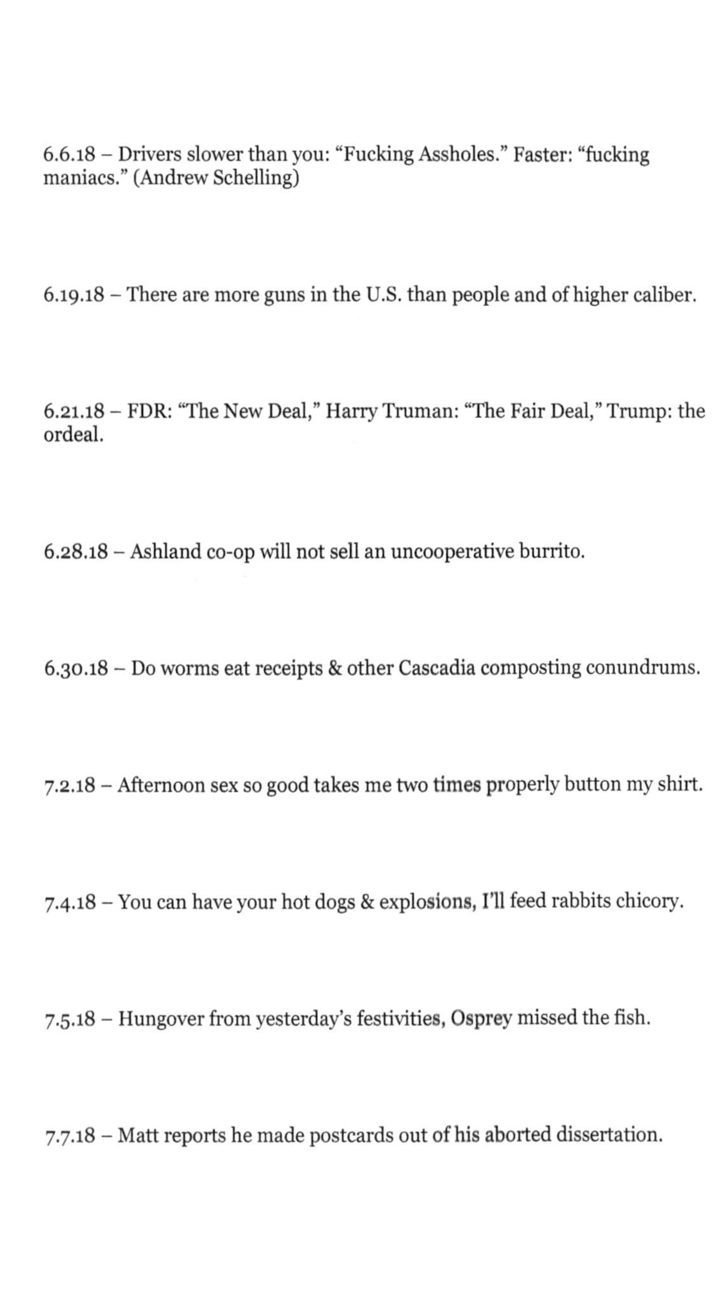

6.6.18 – Drivers slower than you: "Fucking Assholes." Faster: "fucking maniacs." (Andrew Schelling)

6.19.18 – There are more guns in the U.S. than people and of higher caliber.

6.21.18 – FDR: "The New Deal," Harry Truman: "The Fair Deal," Trump: the ordeal.

6.28.18 – Ashland co-op will not sell an uncooperative burrito.

6.30.18 – Do worms eat receipts & other Cascadia composting conundrums.

7.2.18 – Afternoon sex so good takes me two times properly button my shirt.

7.4.18 – You can have your hot dogs & explosions, I'll feed rabbits chicory.

7.5.18 – Hungover from yesterday's festivities, Osprey missed the fish.

7.7.18 – Matt reports he made postcards out of his aborted dissertation.

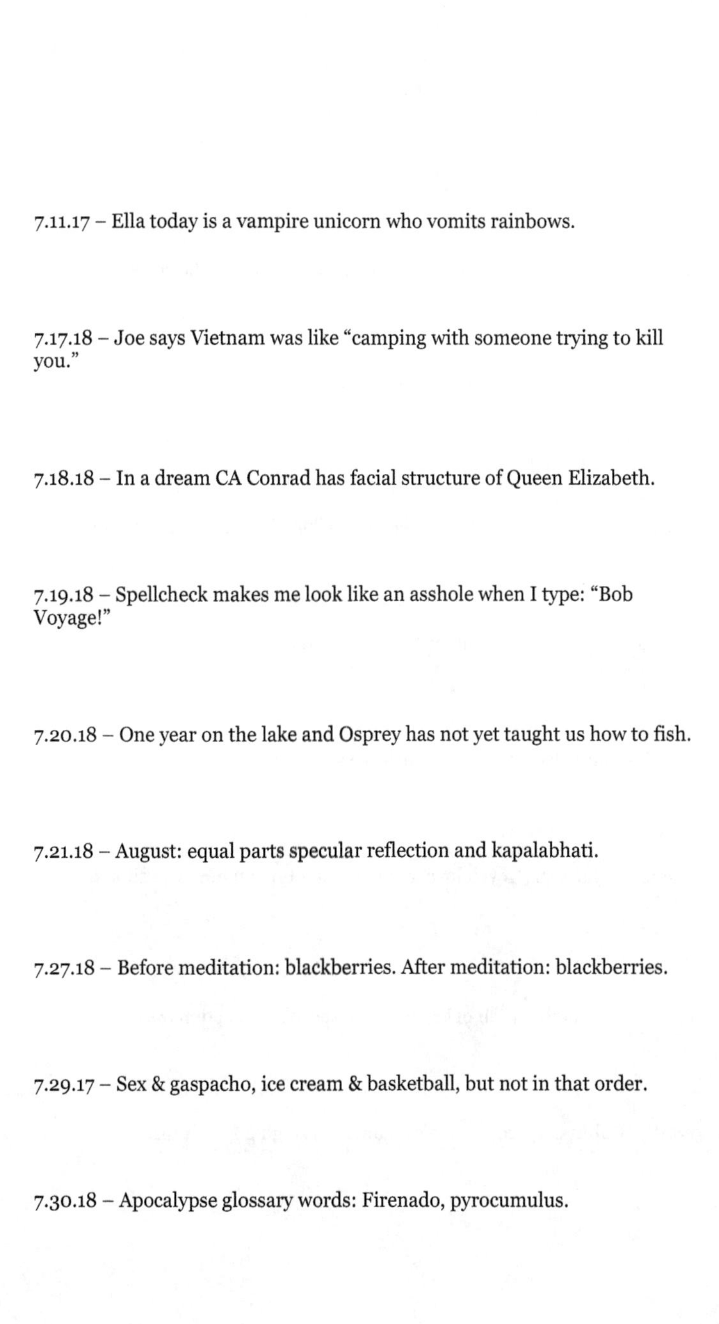

7.11.17 – Ella today is a vampire unicorn who vomits rainbows.

7.17.18 – Joe says Vietnam was like “camping with someone trying to kill you.”

7.18.18 – In a dream CA Conrad has facial structure of Queen Elizabeth.

7.19.18 – Spellcheck makes me look like an asshole when I type: “Bob Voyage!”

7.20.18 – One year on the lake and Osprey has not yet taught us how to fish.

7.21.18 – August: equal parts specular reflection and kapalabhati.

7.27.18 – Before meditation: blackberries. After meditation: blackberries.

7.29.17 – Sex & gaspacho, ice cream & basketball, but not in that order.

7.30.18 – Apocalypse glossary words: Firenado, pyrocumulus.

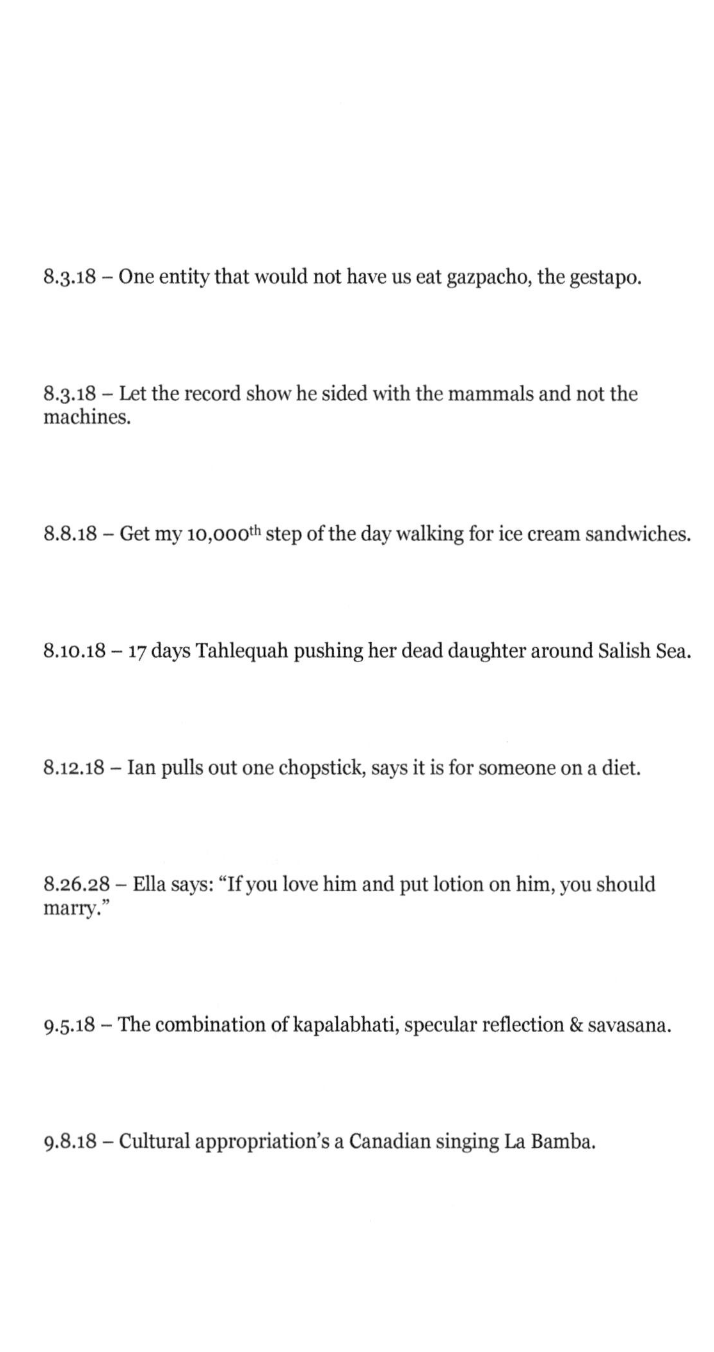

8.3.18 – One entity that would not have us eat gazpacho, the gestapo.

8.3.18 – Let the record show he sided with the mammals and not the machines.

8.8.18 – Get my 10,000th step of the day walking for ice cream sandwiches.

8.10.18 – 17 days Tahlequah pushing her dead daughter around Salish Sea.

8.12.18 – Ian pulls out one chopstick, says it is for someone on a diet.

8.26.28 – Ella says: “If you love him and put lotion on him, you should marry.”

9.5.18 – The combination of kapalabhati, specular reflection & savasana.

9.8.18 – Cultural appropriation’s a Canadian singing La Bamba.

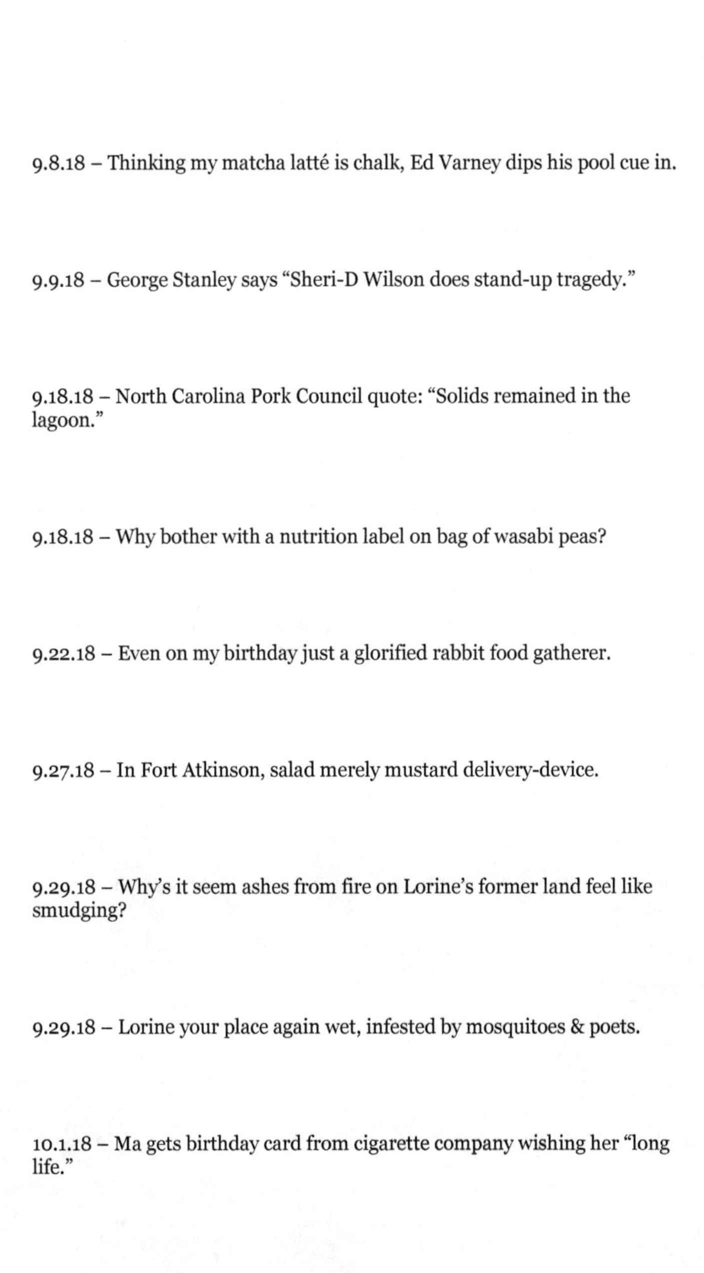

9.8.18 – Thinking my matcha latté is chalk, Ed Varney dips his pool cue in.

9.9.18 – George Stanley says "Sheri-D Wilson does stand-up tragedy."

9.18.18 – North Carolina Pork Council quote: "Solids remained in the lagoon."

9.18.18 – Why bother with a nutrition label on bag of wasabi peas?

9.22.18 – Even on my birthday just a glorified rabbit food gatherer.

9.27.18 – In Fort Atkinson, salad merely mustard delivery-device.

9.29.18 – Why's it seem ashes from fire on Lorine's former land feel like smudging?

9.29.18 – Lorine your place again wet, infested by mosquitoes & poets.

10.1.18 – Ma gets birthday card from cigarette company wishing her "long life."

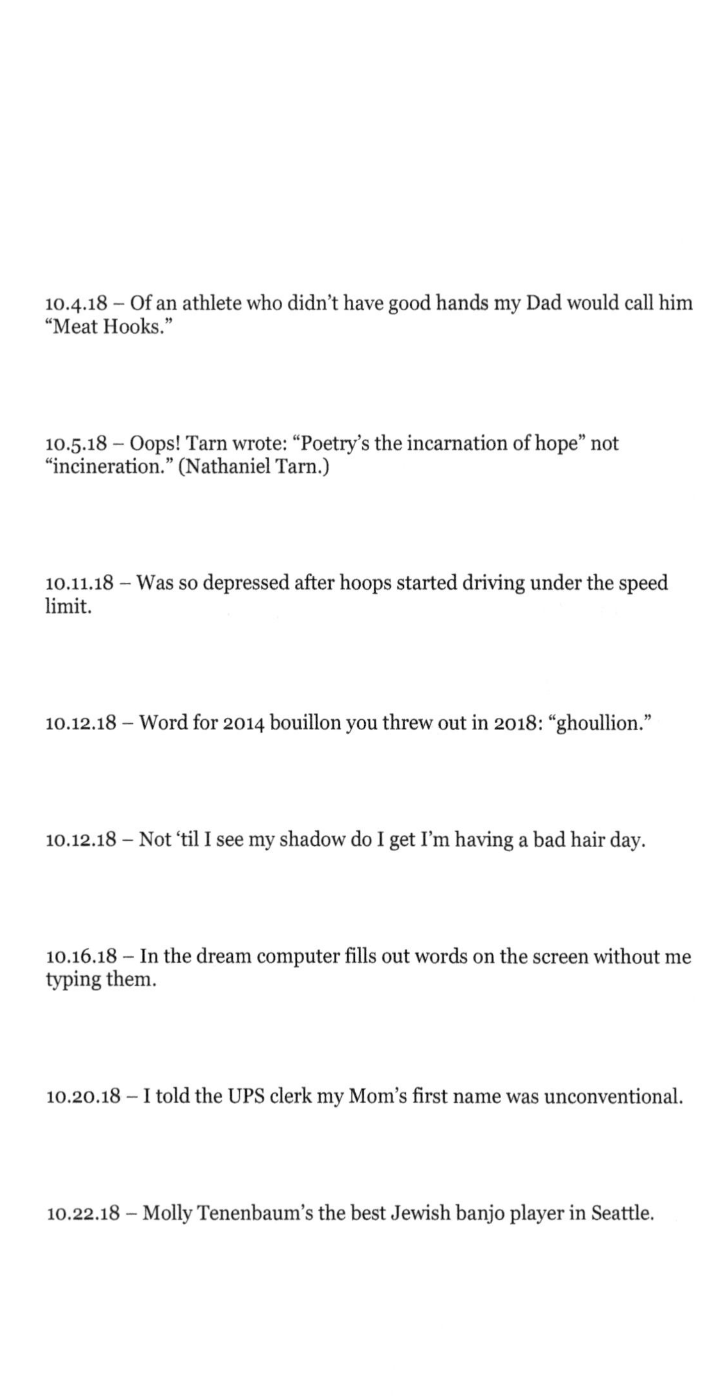

10.4.18 – Of an athlete who didn't have good hands my Dad would call him "Meat Hooks."

10.5.18 – Oops! Tarn wrote: "Poetry's the incarnation of hope" not "incineration." (Nathaniel Tarn.)

10.11.18 – Was so depressed after hoops started driving under the speed limit.

10.12.18 – Word for 2014 bouillon you threw out in 2018: "ghoullion."

10.12.18 – Not 'til I see my shadow do I get I'm having a bad hair day.

10.16.18 – In the dream computer fills out words on the screen without me typing them.

10.20.18 – I told the UPS clerk my Mom's first name was unconventional.

10.22.18 – Molly Tenenbaum's the best Jewish banjo player in Seattle.

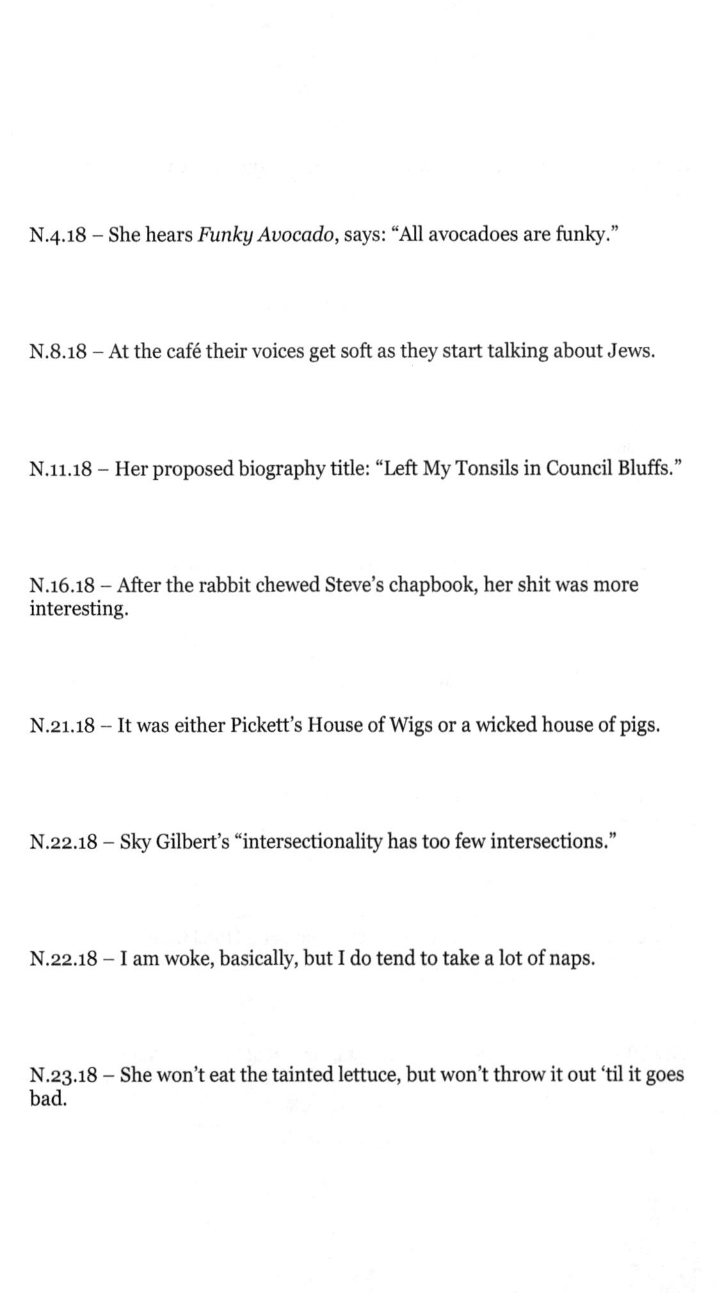

N.4.18 – She hears *Funky Avocado*, says: “All avocadoes are funky.”

N.8.18 – At the café their voices get soft as they start talking about Jews.

N.11.18 – Her proposed biography title: “Left My Tonsils in Council Bluffs.”

N.16.18 – After the rabbit chewed Steve’s chapbook, her shit was more interesting.

N.21.18 – It was either Pickett’s House of Wigs or a wicked house of pigs.

N.22.18 – Sky Gilbert’s “intersectionality has too few intersections.”

N.22.18 – I am woke, basically, but I do tend to take a lot of naps.

N.23.18 – She won’t eat the tainted lettuce, but won’t throw it out ‘til it goes bad.

N.23.18 – Tell Dennis Held: “Stay out of trouble” and he says: “I’ll start tomorrow.”

N.24.18 – Linda Resca, ever try Fresca, putanesca or mescaline?

N.26.18 – Jason encouraging moss growth in his garden / buttermilk smoothies.

N.27.18 – The curse of having a good ear in an age where nobody listens.

N.29.18 – *Gullibility’s a sign of creativity* I said and she believed that too!

12.1.18 – Ella says: “These are the BEST PANCAKES EVER” – then she eats half of one.

12.3.18 – Open mic’s extended – kitchen radio plays Hotel California.

12.14.18 – SPLAB is 25 years of gangsters, Jews & at least one douchebag.

2019

1.4.19 – No concern for climate change said the January rhododendron.

1.6.19 – One duck in the lake to another: "Who you callin' a bufflehead?!?"

1.9.19 – The office of Dr. Forest and Dr. Woods needs a nurse log.

1.13.19 – Shoulda told that Airbnb vegan there's a pork rind on every pillow.

1.14.19 – I know, drugs, surgery & radiation and edit your poems.

1.16.19 – The Stranger: porn, weed ads & stories about pot suppositories.

1.28.19 – Forget basketball – Matt Trease can pull a muscle doing erasures.

2.5.19 – Little puffs of breath (freezing winter day) at tip of hummingbird's beak.

2.12.19 – I hope my sneezing & farting's not affecting your meditation.

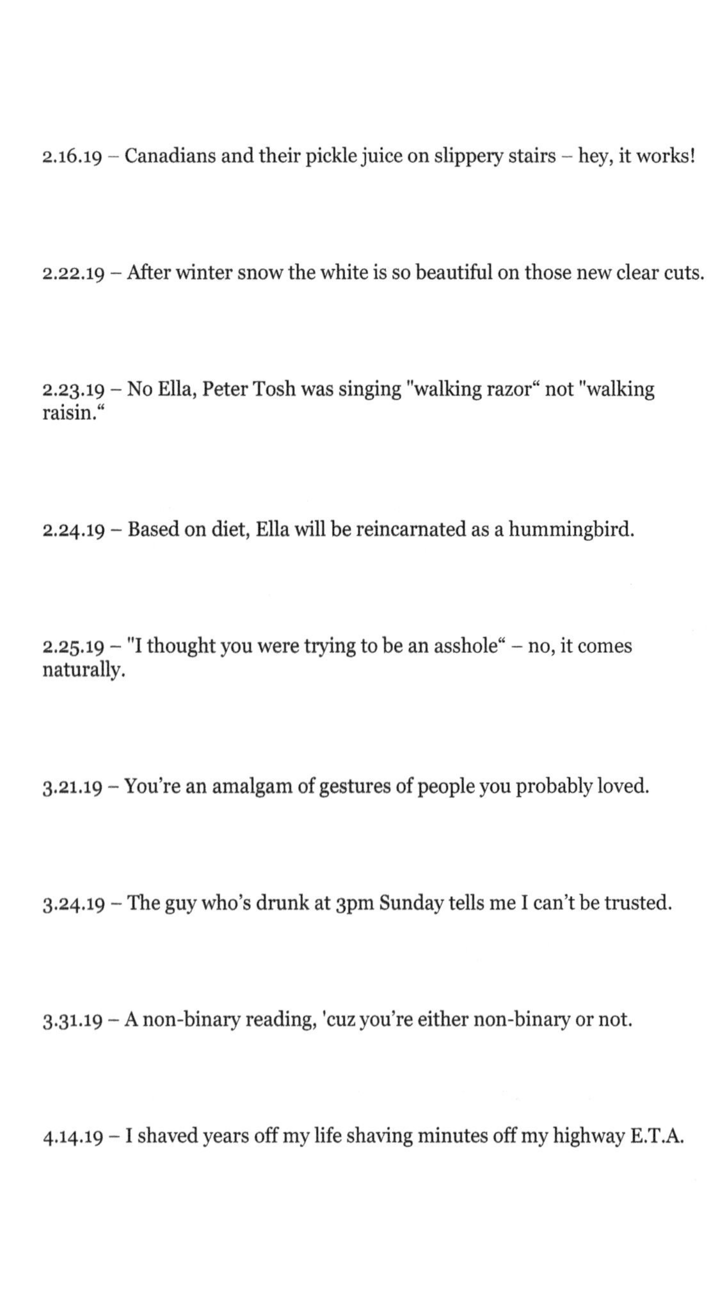

2.16.19 – Canadians and their pickle juice on slippery stairs – hey, it works!

2.22.19 – After winter snow the white is so beautiful on those new clear cuts.

2.23.19 – No Ella, Peter Tosh was singing "walking razor“ not "walking raisin.“

2.24.19 – Based on diet, Ella will be reincarnated as a hummingbird.

2.25.19 – "I thought you were trying to be an asshole“ – no, it comes naturally.

3.21.19 – You're an amalgam of gestures of people you probably loved.

3.24.19 – The guy who's drunk at 3pm Sunday tells me I can't be trusted.

3.31.19 – A non-binary reading, 'cuz you're either non-binary or not.

4.14.19 – I shaved years off my life shaving minutes off my highway E.T.A.

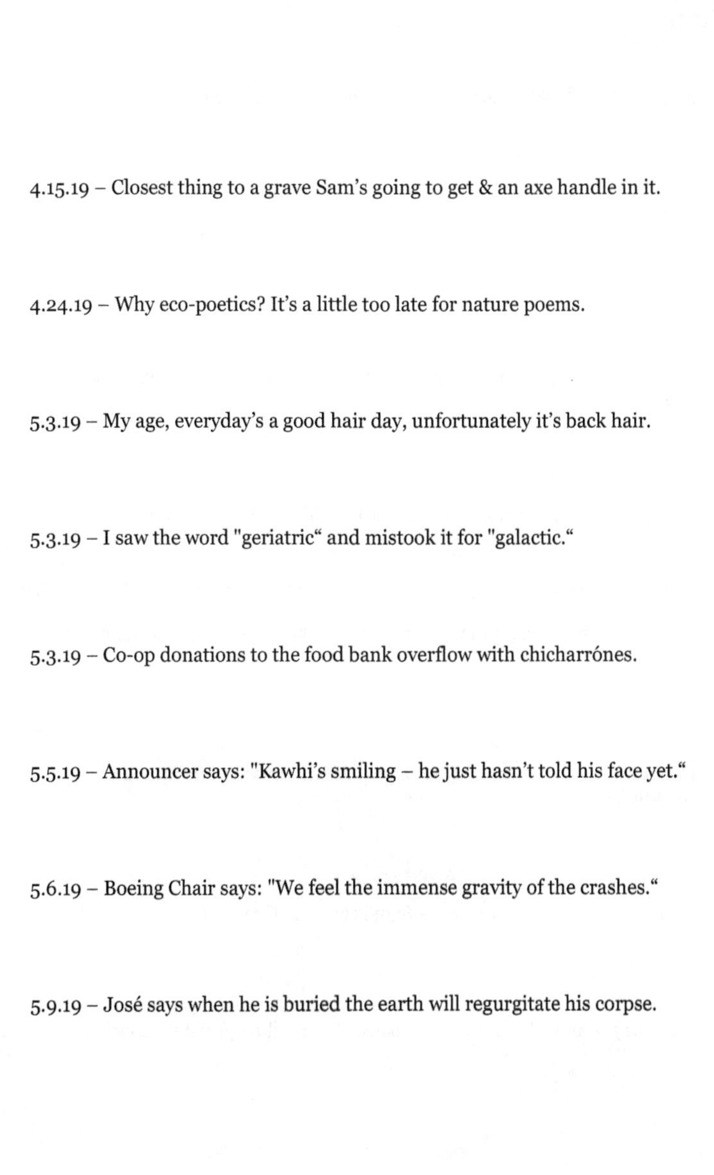

4.15.19 – Closest thing to a grave Sam's going to get & an axe handle in it.

4.24.19 – Why eco-poetics? It's a little too late for nature poems.

5.3.19 – My age, everyday's a good hair day, unfortunately it's back hair.

5.3.19 – I saw the word "geriatric" and mistook it for "galactic."

5.3.19 – Co-op donations to the food bank overflow with chicharrónes.

5.5.19 – Announcer says: "Kawhi's smiling – he just hasn't told his face yet."

5.6.19 – Boeing Chair says: "We feel the immense gravity of the crashes."

5.9.19 – José says when he is buried the earth will regurgitate his corpse.

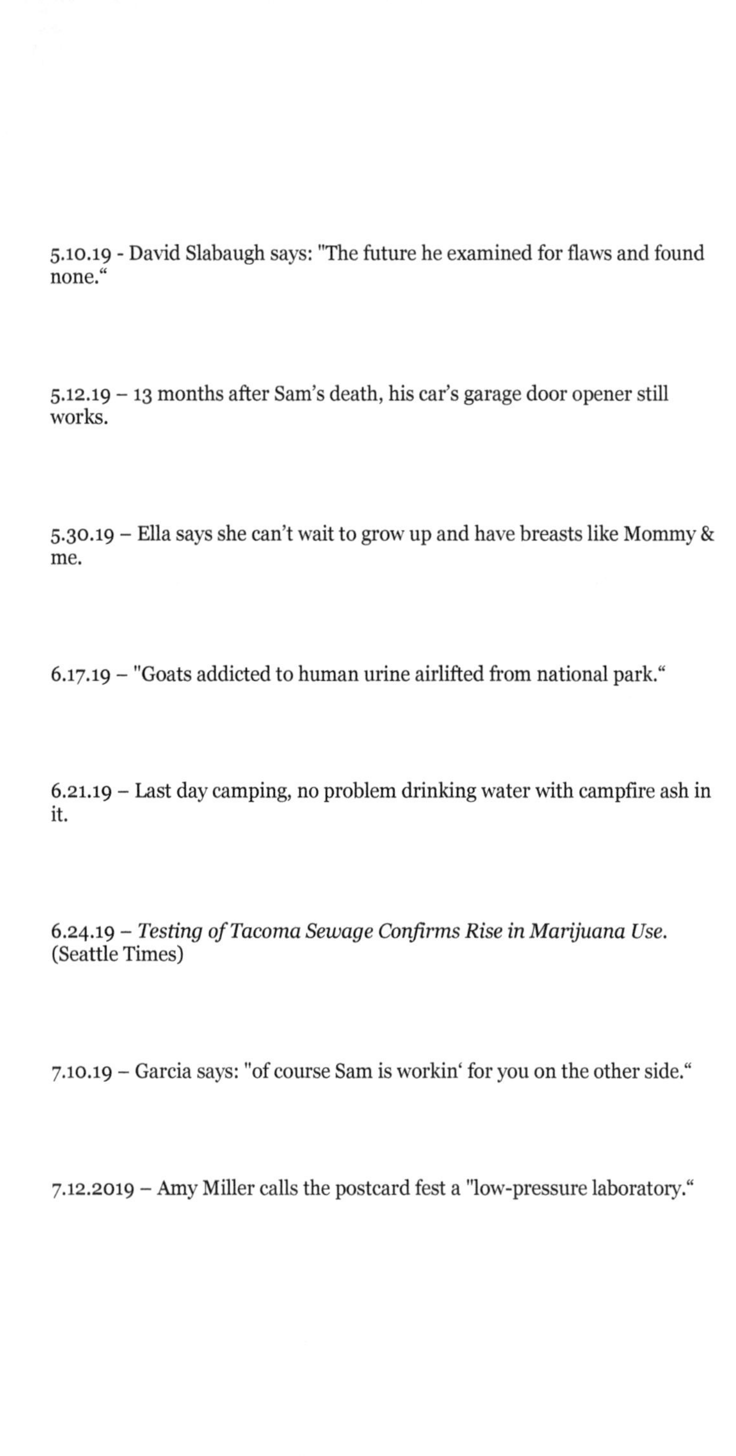

5.10.19 - David Slabaugh says: "The future he examined for flaws and found none."

5.12.19 – 13 months after Sam's death, his car's garage door opener still works.

5.30.19 – Ella says she can't wait to grow up and have breasts like Mommy & me.

6.17.19 – "Goats addicted to human urine airlifted from national park."

6.21.19 – Last day camping, no problem drinking water with campfire ash in it.

6.24.19 – *Testing of Tacoma Sewage Confirms Rise in Marijuana Use.* (Seattle Times)

7.10.19 – Garcia says: "of course Sam is workin' for you on the other side."

7.12.2019 – Amy Miller calls the postcard fest a "low-pressure laboratory."

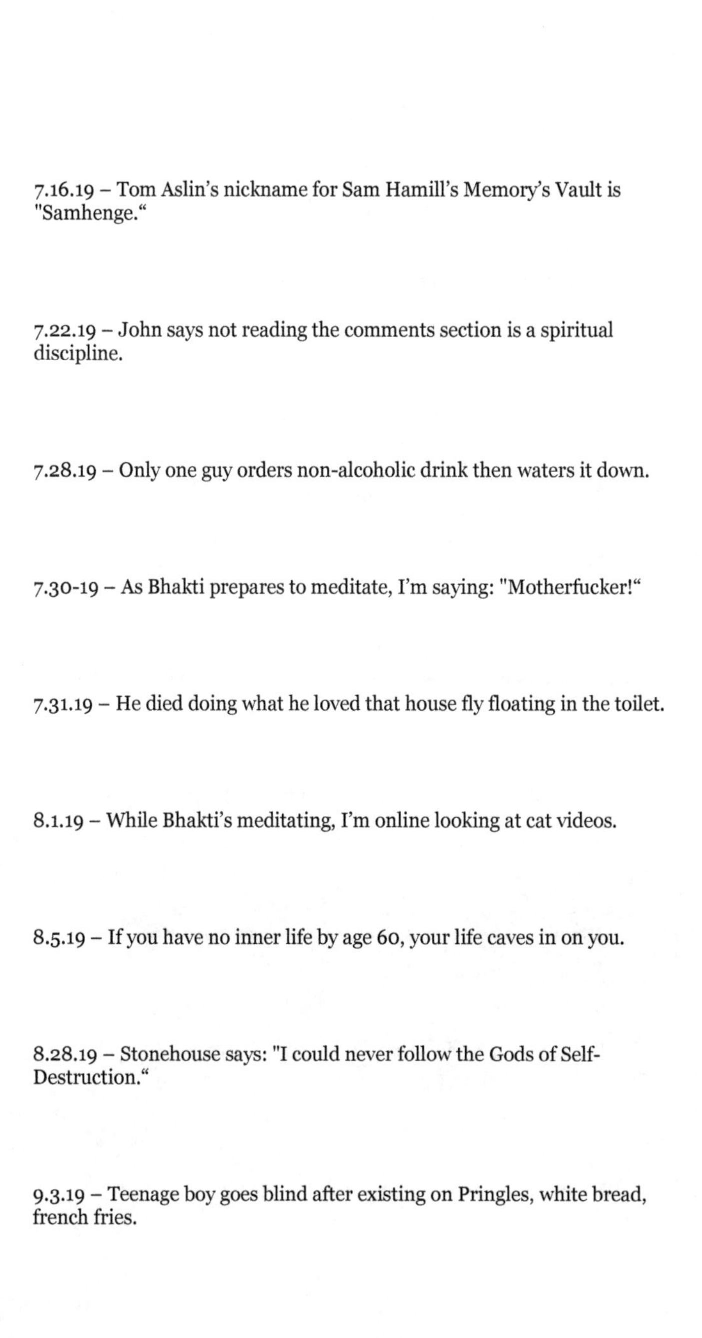

7.16.19 – Tom Aslin's nickname for Sam Hamill's Memory's Vault is "Samhenge."

7.22.19 – John says not reading the comments section is a spiritual discipline.

7.28.19 – Only one guy orders non-alcoholic drink then waters it down.

7.30-19 – As Bhakti prepares to meditate, I'm saying: "Motherfucker!"

7.31.19 – He died doing what he loved that house fly floating in the toilet.

8.1.19 – While Bhakti's meditating, I'm online looking at cat videos.

8.5.19 – If you have no inner life by age 60, your life caves in on you.

8.28.19 – Stonehouse says: "I could never follow the Gods of Self-Destruction."

9.3.19 – Teenage boy goes blind after existing on Pringles, white bread, french fries.

9.7.19 – Dream someone's running the dishwasher but I'm camping by the river.

9.7.19 – We are on loan from the miracle and the miracle is butter.

9.12.19 – Meat/Meteor/Meatiest, Tear/Terrier/Terrorist, Eight/Eighthier/Athiest.

9.12.19 – Cascadia where they give their dogs CBD during thunderstorms.

9.18.19 – Next Door Neighbor logic: "People don't kill people, bike lanes kill people."

9.22.19 – Meticulous he cleans airplane seat & tray to watch violent films.

10.27.19 – We need to have diets less like turkey vultures and more like rabbits.

N.5.19 – We have the technology to blow leaves into the next galaxy.

N.13.19 – Did I join Tik Tok to see someone fling sliced cheese out his car window?

N.14.19 – It's clear to me thinly-sliced bread is the best invention since sliced bread.

N.15.19 – Goodbye dear Judith. In heaven I am sure they'll save you some cocaine.

N.15.19 – Bhakti's an end of life doula, but with her I prefer petit mort.

N.18.19 – Tige says the only word you can't use in a poem is "cocksucker."

N.19.19 – Ella does not like fish, but loves hamachi sashimi and unagi.

N.20.19 – Judith Roche: "I believe in all the gods, I just don't like some of them."

N.23.19 – She writes a poem every seven years no matter how much it hurts.

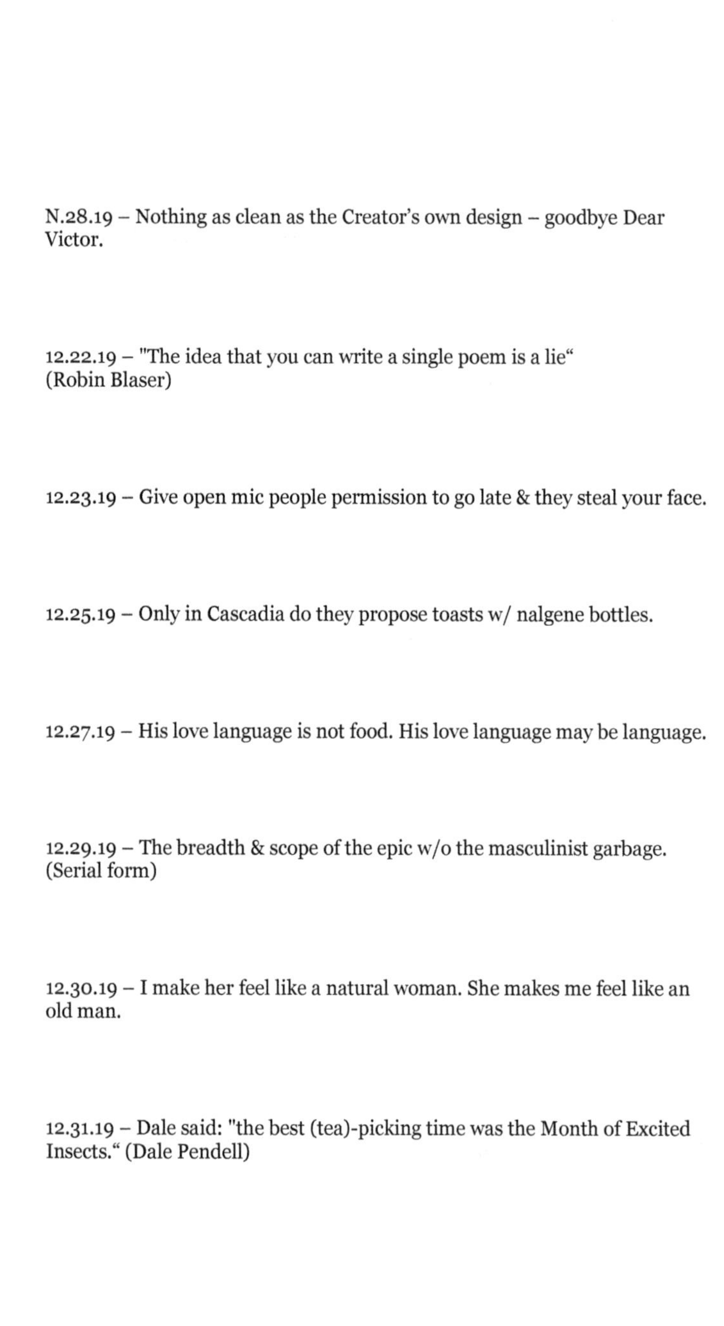

N.28.19 – Nothing as clean as the Creator's own design – goodbye Dear Victor.

12.22.19 – "The idea that you can write a single poem is a lie"
(Robin Blaser)

12.23.19 – Give open mic people permission to go late & they steal your face.

12.25.19 – Only in Cascadia do they propose toasts w/ nalgene bottles.

12.27.19 – His love language is not food. His love language may be language.

12.29.19 – The breadth & scope of the epic w/o the masculinist garbage.
(Serial form)

12.30.19 – I make her feel like a natural woman. She makes me feel like an old man.

12.31.19 – Dale said: "the best (tea)-picking time was the Month of Excited Insects." (Dale Pendell)

2020

1.3.20 – "Death's comprised of deep blue tortures" says McClure, mouth full of chocolate cake.

1.5.20 – Octogenarian's Latihan sounds like practice to be a ghost.

1.13.20 – Gwyneth Paltrow is selling a candle that smells like her vagina.

1.21.20 – Renée says at the wedding Rebecca Rose "cried her eyelashes off."

1.22.20 – Comiendo aire Kozer says, Chronic Hyperventilation Syndrome.

1.23.20 – Bhakti says there are no spinsters anymore just crazy cat ladies.

1.24.20 – "Gout" I tell her & Barb laughs & says: "Isn't that a rich man's disease?"

1.25.20 – Happy New Year of The Rat I Hope You Get Rich You Metal Ox!

1.29.20 – At least the two leaf blowers are blowing in the exact same key.

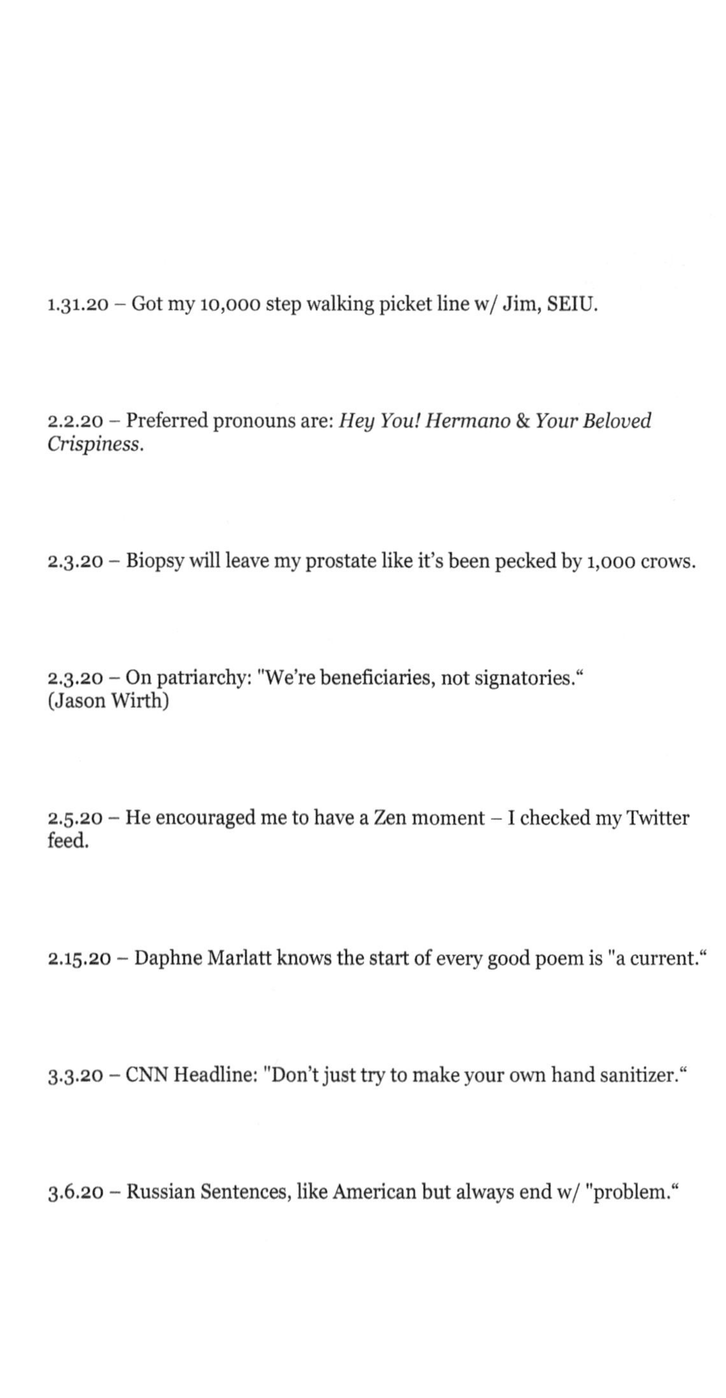

1.31.20 – Got my 10,000 step walking picket line w/ Jim, SEIU.

2.2.20 – Preferred pronouns are: *Hey You! Hermano* & *Your Beloved Crispiness.*

2.3.20 – Biopsy will leave my prostate like it's been pecked by 1,000 crows.

2.3.20 – On patriarchy: "We're beneficiaries, not signatories."
(Jason Wirth)

2.5.20 – He encouraged me to have a Zen moment – I checked my Twitter feed.

2.15.20 – Daphne Marlatt knows the start of every good poem is "a current."

3.3.20 – CNN Headline: "Don't just try to make your own hand sanitizer."

3.6.20 – Russian Sentences, like American but always end w/ "problem."

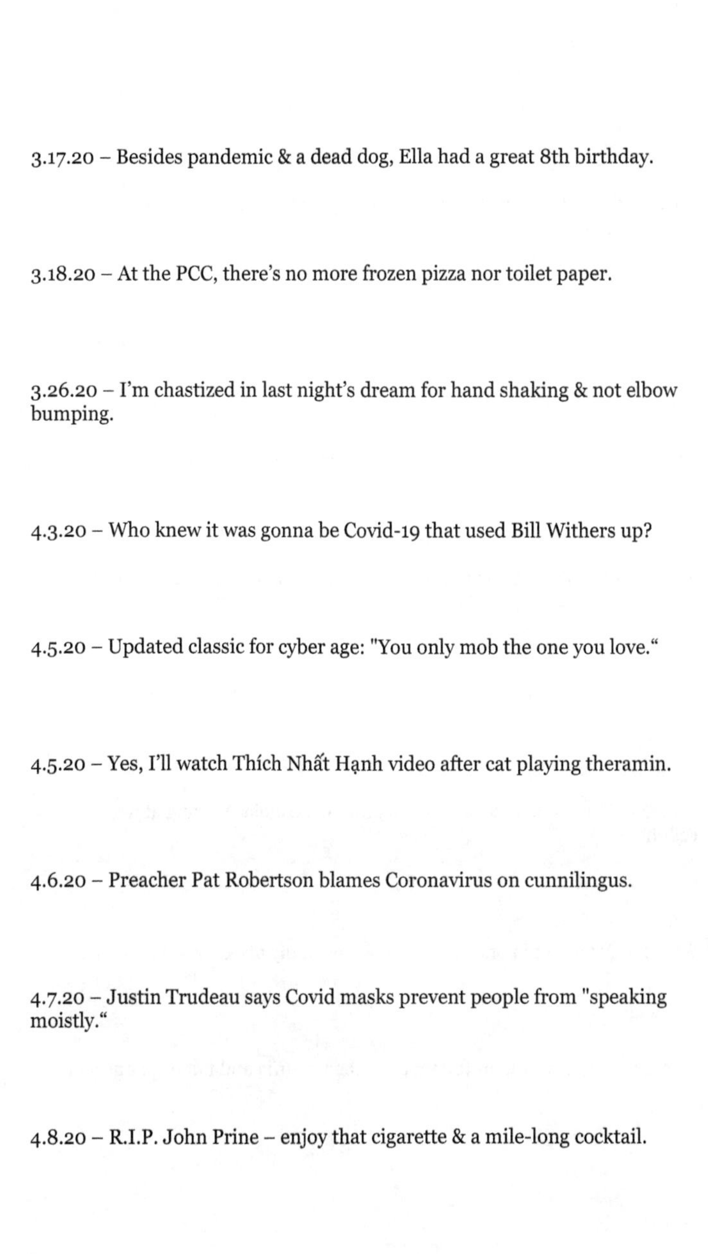

3.17.20 – Besides pandemic & a dead dog, Ella had a great 8th birthday.

3.18.20 – At the PCC, there's no more frozen pizza nor toilet paper.

3.26.20 – I'm chastized in last night's dream for hand shaking & not elbow bumping.

4.3.20 – Who knew it was gonna be Covid-19 that used Bill Withers up?

4.5.20 – Updated classic for cyber age: "You only mob the one you love.“

4.5.20 – Yes, I'll watch Thích Nhất Hạnh video after cat playing theramin.

4.6.20 – Preacher Pat Robertson blames Coronavirus on cunnilingus.

4.7.20 – Justin Trudeau says Covid masks prevent people from "speaking moistly.“

4.8.20 – R.I.P. John Prine – enjoy that cigarette & a mile-long cocktail.

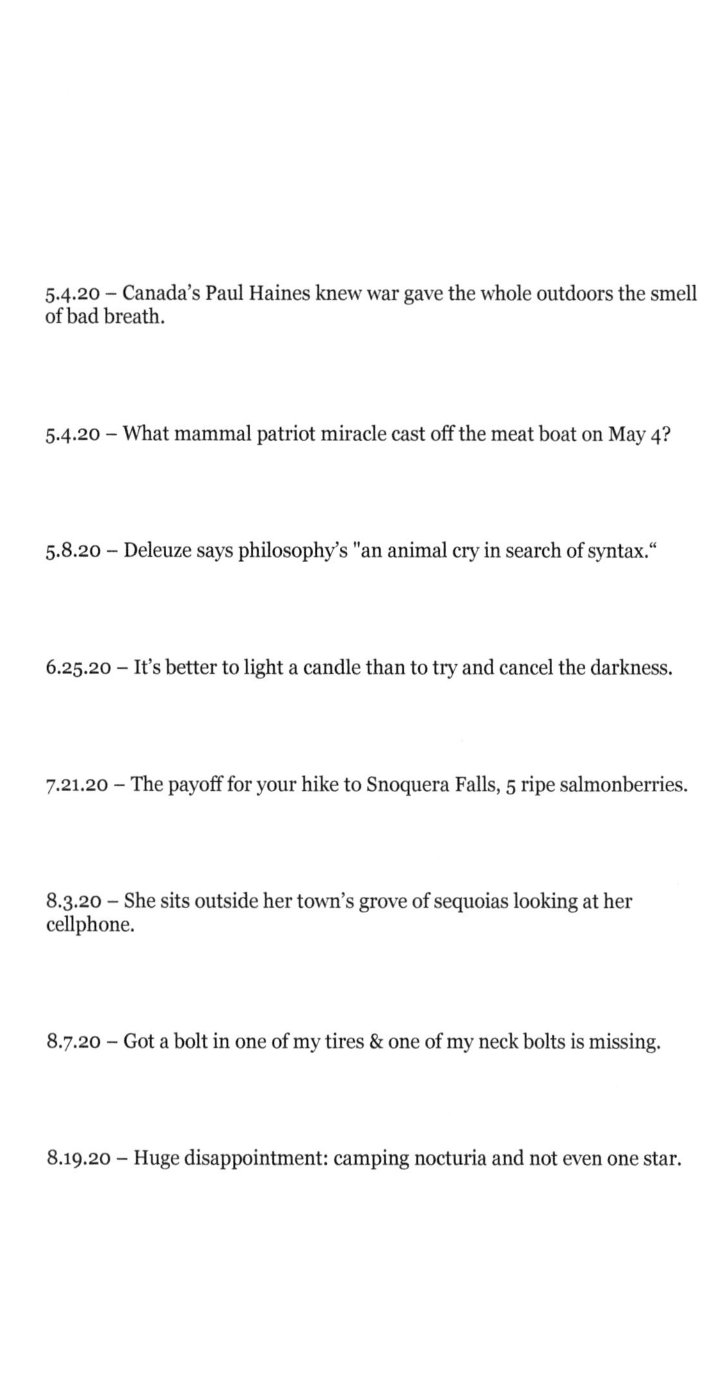

5.4.20 – Canada's Paul Haines knew war gave the whole outdoors the smell of bad breath.

5.4.20 – What mammal patriot miracle cast off the meat boat on May 4?

5.8.20 – Deleuze says philosophy's "an animal cry in search of syntax."

6.25.20 – It's better to light a candle than to try and cancel the darkness.

7.21.20 – The payoff for your hike to Snoquera Falls, 5 ripe salmonberries.

8.3.20 – She sits outside her town's grove of sequoias looking at her cellphone.

8.7.20 – Got a bolt in one of my tires & one of my neck bolts is missing.

8.19.20 – Huge disappointment: camping nocturia and not even one star.

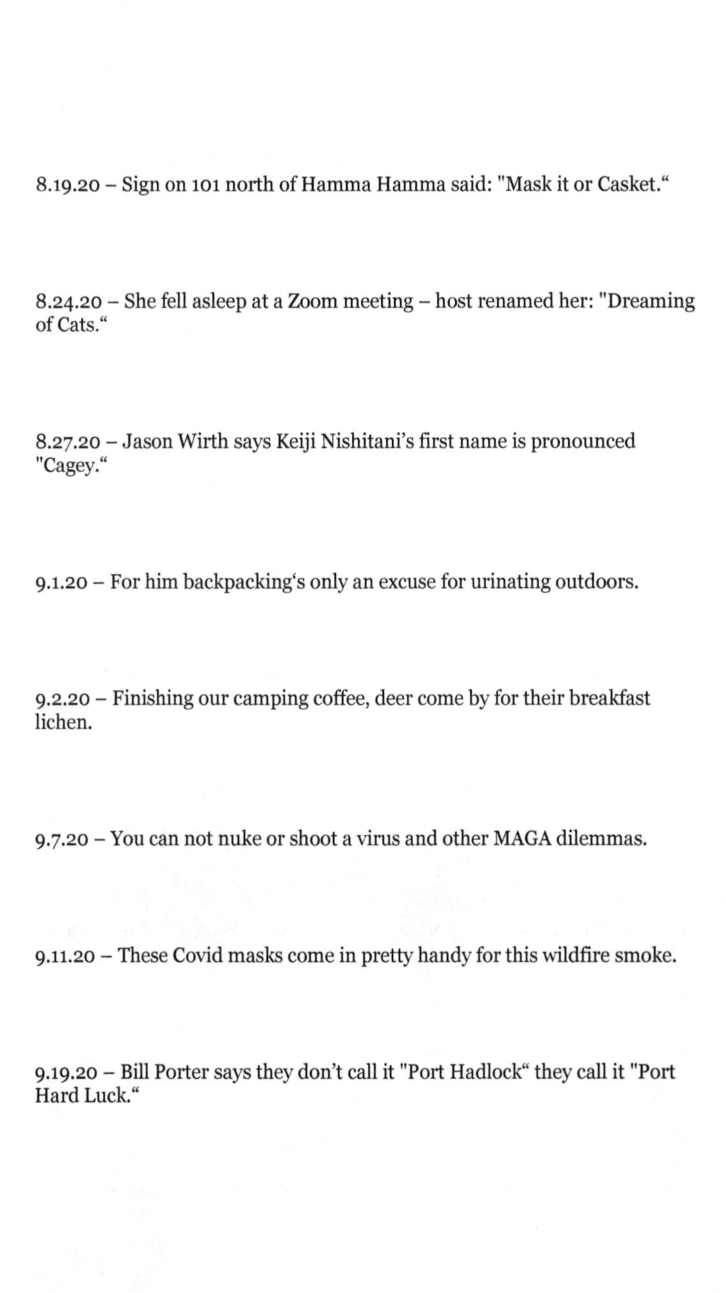

8.19.20 – Sign on 101 north of Hamma Hamma said: "Mask it or Casket.“

8.24.20 – She fell asleep at a Zoom meeting – host renamed her: "Dreaming of Cats.“

8.27.20 – Jason Wirth says Keiji Nishitani’s first name is pronounced "Cagey.“

9.1.20 – For him backpacking‘s only an excuse for urinating outdoors.

9.2.20 – Finishing our camping coffee, deer come by for their breakfast lichen.

9.7.20 – You can not nuke or shoot a virus and other MAGA dilemmas.

9.11.20 – These Covid masks come in pretty handy for this wildfire smoke.

9.19.20 – Bill Porter says they don’t call it "Port Hadlock“ they call it "Port Hard Luck.“

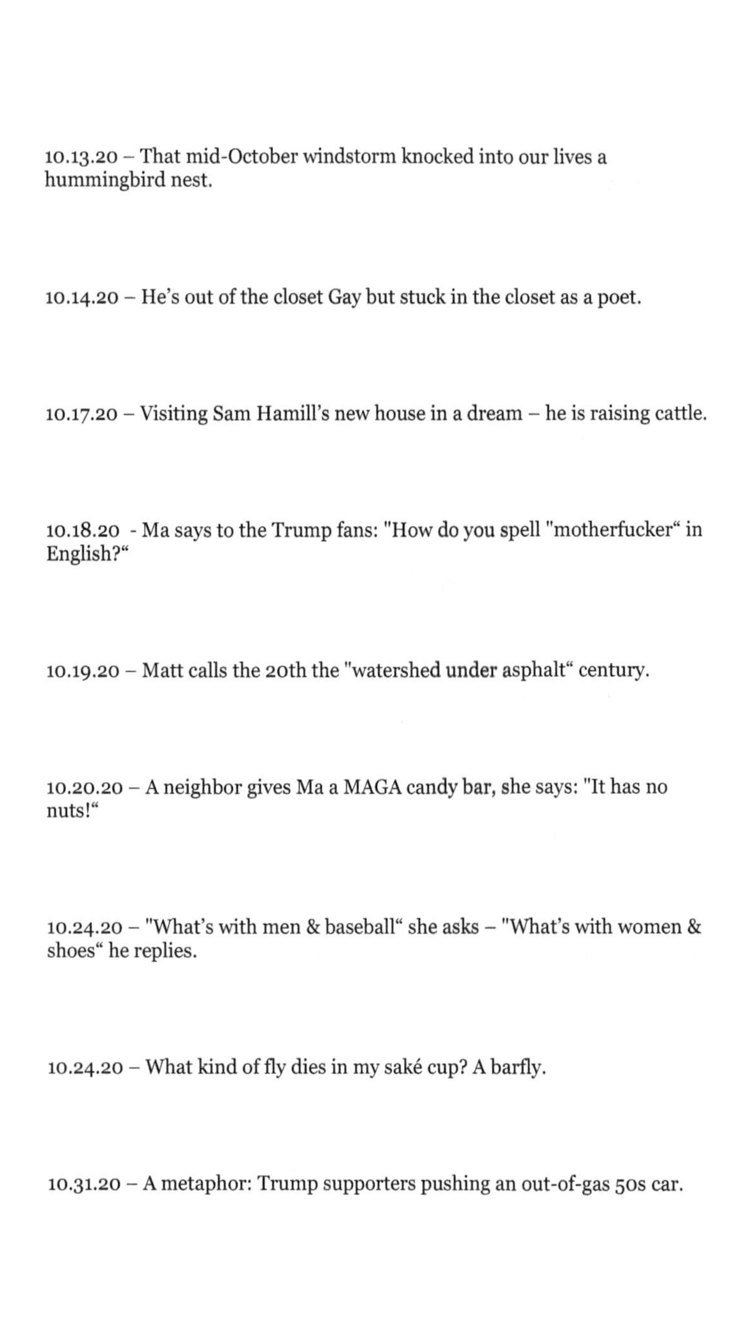

10.13.20 – That mid-October windstorm knocked into our lives a hummingbird nest.

10.14.20 – He's out of the closet Gay but stuck in the closet as a poet.

10.17.20 – Visiting Sam Hamill's new house in a dream – he is raising cattle.

10.18.20 - Ma says to the Trump fans: "How do you spell "motherfucker“ in English?“

10.19.20 – Matt calls the 20th the "watershed under asphalt“ century.

10.20.20 – A neighbor gives Ma a MAGA candy bar, she says: "It has no nuts!“

10.24.20 – "What's with men & baseball“ she asks – "What's with women & shoes“ he replies.

10.24.20 – What kind of fly dies in my saké cup? A barfly.

10.31.20 – A metaphor: Trump supporters pushing an out-of-gas 50s car.

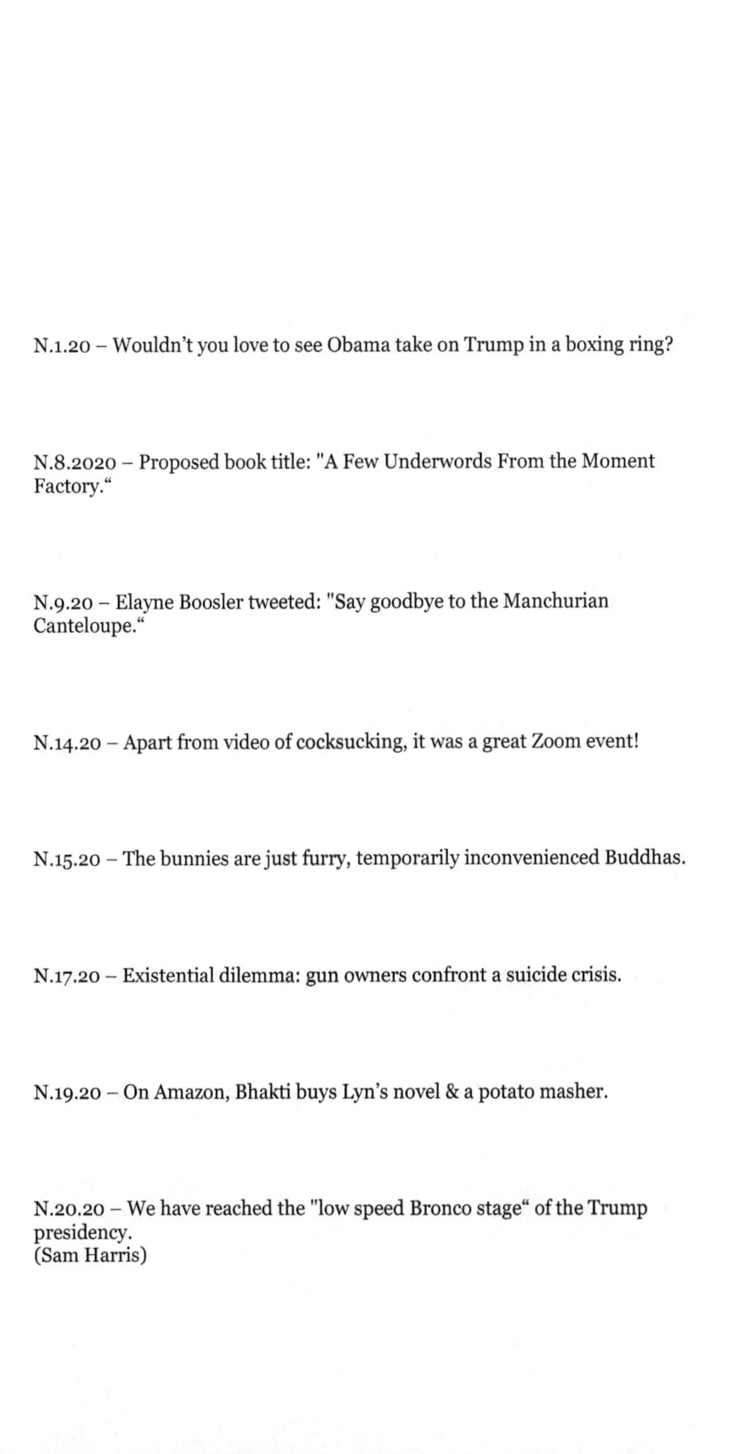

N.1.20 – Wouldn't you love to see Obama take on Trump in a boxing ring?

N.8.2020 – Proposed book title: "A Few Underwords From the Moment Factory."

N.9.20 – Elayne Boosler tweeted: "Say goodbye to the Manchurian Canteloupe."

N.14.20 – Apart from video of cocksucking, it was a great Zoom event!

N.15.20 – The bunnies are just furry, temporarily inconvenienced Buddhas.

N.17.20 – Existential dilemma: gun owners confront a suicide crisis.

N.19.20 – On Amazon, Bhakti buys Lyn's novel & a potato masher.

N.20.20 – We have reached the "low speed Bronco stage" of the Trump presidency.
(Sam Harris)

N.22.20 – I thought today Don King would reincarnate as a Kingfisher.

N.29.20 – Start to like the poem until I realize it's a SESTINA!

12.2.20 – James said: "Gay men did not march for Korean orphans & lawn mowers!"
(James Gaynor)

12.3.20 – What's real and what's just a rotating stumble of meaty cravings?

12.13.20 – Somebody else's spellcheck masterpiece: "How the Gringo Stole Christmas."

12.15.20 – Your yoga pants collection is not indicative of an inner life.

12.20.20 – Never not notice processions at the heart of a planet's thinking.

12.27.20 – She doesn't think: "I got tired of shaving" would make a good epitaph.

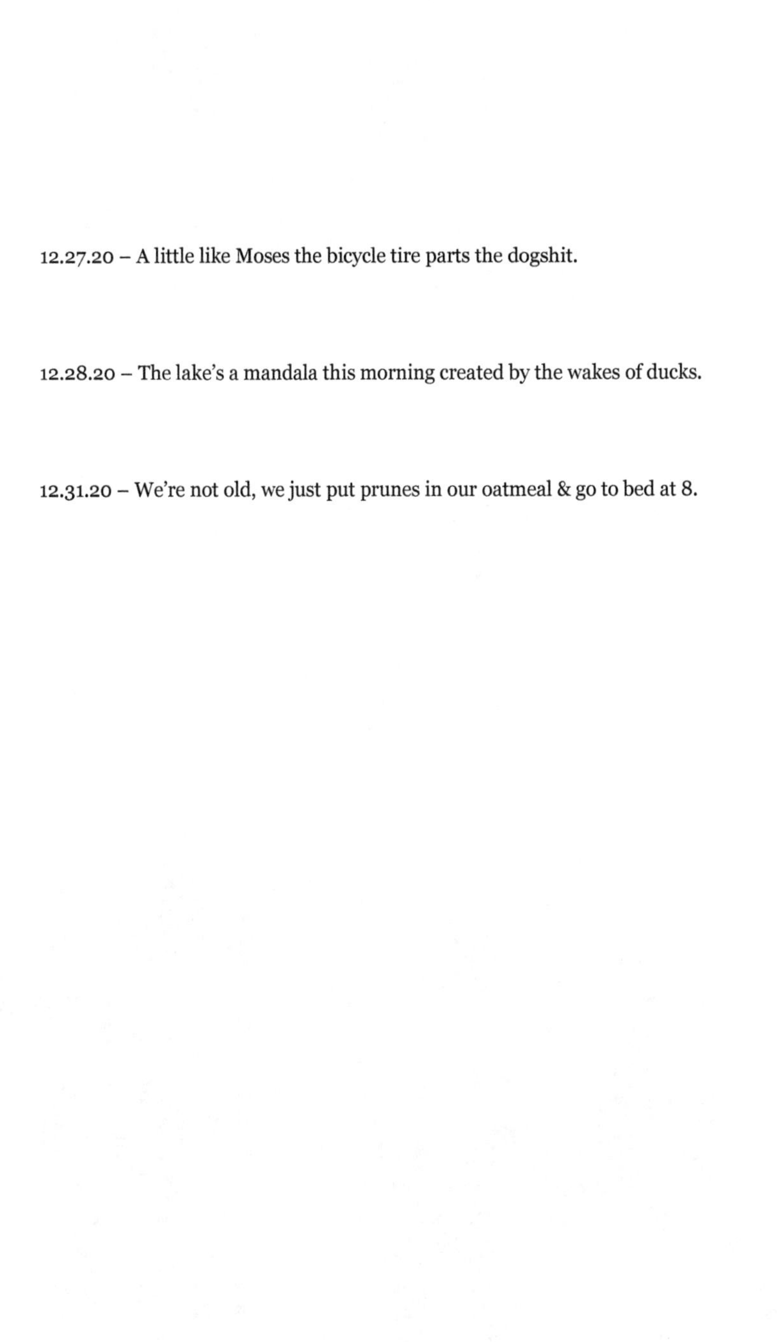

12.27.20 – A little like Moses the bicycle tire parts the dogshit.

12.28.20 – The lake's a mandala this morning created by the wakes of ducks.

12.31.20 – We're not old, we just put prunes in our oatmeal & go to bed at 8.

2021

1.1.21 – 2020 was taken out to the alley & shot in the head.

Works Cited

Ginsberg, Allen. *Cosmopolitan Greetings*. New York: Harper Collins, 1994.

Hoffman, Yoel. *Japanese Death Poems*. Boston: Turtle Publishing, 1986.

McClure, Michael. *Scratching the Beat Surface*. New York: Penguin, 1994.

Olson, Charles, *Collected Prose*. Berkeley: University of California Press, 1997.

Schelling, Andrew, and Anne Waldman. Personal interview. April, 2001.

http://www.americansentences.com

About Paul E. Nelson

Poet and interviewer Paul E. Nelson founded Cascadia Poetics Lab (formerly SPLAB) & the Cascadia Poetry Festival. He wrote *A Time Before Slaughter* (shortlisted for a 2010 Genius Award by The Stranger) and a second edition in 2020 which includes a new section of his ongoing serial poem entitled: *Pig War: & Other Songs of Cascadia* and also: *American Prophets: Interviews 1994-2012*, and *Organic in Cascadia: A Sequence of Energies* (book-length-essay, Lumme Editions, Brazil, 2013). Forthcoming in 2022: *Haibun De la Serna*. He's interviewed Allen Ginsberg, Joanne Kyger, Micheal McClure, Sam Hamill, Brenda Hillman, José Kozer, Diane di Prima, Robin Blaser, Nate Mackey, George Bowering and Daphne Marlatt; presented poetry/poetics in London, Brussels, Vancouver, Nanaimo, Qinghai & Beijing, China, and writes an American Sentence every day. Awarded a residency at The Lake, from the Morris Graves Foundation in Loleta, CA, he's been published in *Rattle, Pocket Lint, Journal of the Plague Year, Dispatches from the Poetry Wars*, the *For Love of Orcas* anthology, the *South Seattle Emerald, Golden Handcuffs Review, Zen Monster, Hambone*, won the 2014 Robin Blaser Award from the *Capilano Review* and lives in the Cedar River watershed in the Cascadia bioregion with Bhakti Watts & youngest daughter Ella Roque. www.PaulENelson.com

Apprentice House is the country's only campus-based, student-staffed book publishing company. Directed by professors and industry professionals, it is a nonprofit activity of the Communication Department at Loyola University Maryland.

Using state-of-the-art technology and an experiential learning model of education, Apprentice House publishes books in untraditional ways. This dual responsibility as publishers and educators creates an unprecedented collaborative environment among faculty and students, while teaching tomorrow's editors, designers, and marketers.

Outside of class, progress on book projects is carried forth by the AH Book Publishing Club, a co-curricular campus organization supported by Loyola University Maryland's Office of Student Activities.

Eclectic and provocative, Apprentice House titles intend to entertain as well as spark dialogue on a variety of topics. Financial contributions to sustain the press's work are welcomed. Contributions are tax deductible to the fullest extent allowed by the IRS.

To learn more about Apprentice House books or to obtain submission guidelines, please visit www.apprenticehouse.com.

Apprentice House
Communication Department
Loyola University Maryland
4501 N. Charles Street
Baltimore, MD 21210
Ph: 410-617-5265
info@apprenticehouse.com • www.apprenticehouse.com

Printed in the USA
CPSIA information can be obtained
at www.ICGtesting.com
JSHW060548230923
48797JS00013B/203